LYLE

ANTIQUE DEALERS
POCKET GUIDE

Anthony Curtis

A PERIGEE BOOK

Perigee Books
are published by
The Putnam Publishing Group
200 Madison Avenue
New York, NY 10016

The publishers wish to express their sincere thanks to the following for their involvement and assistance in the production of this volume.

Edited by ANTHONY CURTIS

ANNETTE CURTIS	DONNA BONAR
EELIN McIVOR	JACQUELINE LEDDY
TRACEY BLACK	FRANK BURRELL
LOUISE SCOTT-JONES	JAMES BROWN
NICKY FAIRBURN	EILEEN BURRELL
CATRIONA McKINVEN	

Library of Congress Cataloging-in-Publication Data

Curtis, Tony, date.
    [Antique dealers pocket book]
    Antique dealers pocket guide / Tony Curtis.
       p.   cm.
    Originally published: The antique dealers pocket book. Glenmayne,
Galashiels, Selkirkshire : Lyle Publications, c1986.
    "A Perigee book."
    Includes index.
    ISBN 0-399-51852-5
    1. Antiques—Handbooks, manuals, etc.   I. Title.
NK1125.C88   1994   93-42300   CIP
745.1—dc20

Cover design by Jack Ribik
Front cover photograph by Bonhams of London

Printed in the United States of America
1 2 3 4 5 6 7 8 9 10

INTRODUCTION

With the ever increasing popularity of antique collecting, there is a need for a comprehensive reference book containing detailed illustrations — not only of the items which command the highest prices but also those pieces which, although not antiques in the true sense, are much sought after by members of the trade.

Here, in one handy, pocket sized volume, are well over 3,500 clear illustrations to facilitate instant recognition and dating of the host of day to day items which make up the bulk of the antiques market.

Compiled primarily with the professional dealer in view, this book makes inter-trade reference simple and accurate.

Interior decorators too, will find communication with their clients considerably improved through use of this book, once again ensuring that there can be no confusion resulting from verbal descriptions being inaccurately given or incompletely understood.

We are confident that every user of The Antique Dealer's Pocket Guide will find it of invaluable assistance in the smooth running of their business and a useful addition to their works of reference.

Anthony Curtis

DRAWINGS BY

TESSA ARNOLD
JANE BARTON
STUART BARTON
JOANNE BROWN
SUZANNE COLE
BOB CORRALL
SARAH CREASE
MARGARET CURRIE
KAREN DOUGLASS
NICHOLA FAIRBURN
DENISE FREEMEN
PAMELA GRANT
LEN GRAY
ELAINE HARLAND
MARY HAYMAN
GEORGE HOGG
BRIAN HOLTON
PETER KNOX
MARGARET LILLIE
TOM MACKIE
CHRIS MANSELL
JOHN MARTIN
CARMEN MILIVOYEVICH
ALISON MORRISON
RICHARD MUNDAY
JOHN R. NABBS
J. PAGE
ROBERT SUTHERLAND
PETER TENCH
J. B. THOMPSON
NORMA TWEEDIE
W. YOUNG

CONTENTS

CONTENTS

CONTENTS

CONTENTS

AMERICAN PERIODS

PILGRIM STYLE – 17TH CENTURY

This earliest distinguishable American style was derived from Renaissance and 17th century English models. Items were massive, rectilinear and of simple basic construction. Tables were mainly trestle based or gateleg; chairs were comprised often of posts and spindles with rush seats or had hard slat backs. Typical was the Wainscot chair, which, with its solid back and columnar turned legs, was based on Elizabethan models.

WILLIAM & MARY 1690–1725

This style was introduced into America at the end of the 17th century, and was essentially a New World version of the baroque. Chairs had scroll, spiral and columnar legs, surfaces were richly decorated, painted or veneered, and walnut and maple replaced oak as the major working media. Innovations at this time included the butterfly table, and tea and dressing tables also became popular.

QUEEN ANNE 1725–50

This followed the English Queen Anne style, with elegant curving forms. Walnut, cherry and maple were the most popular woods, and mahogany began to be imported from around 1750. Finely decorated candlestands and tea-tables with tripod, cabriole bases are typical of this period, and folding games tables and large, drop-leaf tables also emerged at this time.

CHIPPENDALE 1750–80

This was more conservative than its English counterpart and reflected earlier 18th century trends such as ball and claw feet, which were already démodé in London. Designs were much lighter than those of the Queen Anne period and forms became more ornamental. Intricate chair backs, including the ladder back, now became popular. Mahogany was by now the favored wood.

During this period different regional preferences became apparent. Craftsmen in Newport, Rhode Island, for example, followed the classical style more closely, with fluted and reeded columns and legs, whereas their Philadelphia counterparts produced more elaborately carved rococo pieces.

FEDERAL 1780–1820

This was the American answer to neoclassicism. Most furniture of the period will be described as either Sheraton or Hepplewhite, although it is difficult to establish how much American craftsmen actually depended on their designs. In any case, the suggestion that there is a vast difference between them is also somewhat spurious.

The later Federal period saw a much more literal borrowing of Greco-Roman motifs, and the French influence of the Empire style, whether it came direct or filtered through England, is also apparent. New forms, such as the work table, appeared. Side tables too became popular as did chair backs with a center splat carved with classical motifs such as urn and feather or a series of columns. After 1800, however, chair designs became heavier, while sofa designs became simpler. The Grecian couch found its modern counterpart as a daybed. Duncan Phyfe was one of the best and most sought after exponents of the Federal style.

EMPIRE 1815–40

The delicacy of early neo-classicism gave way now to heavier classical forms with more emphasis on outline than on carved detail. In the Empire style, undulating scrolls typically balanced heavy geometric shapes with ornamentation carved in high relief. Mahogany, rosewood veneers and marble were common materials. A French emigré, Charles Henri Lannuier, was among the first to introduce the style to America in the first years of the 19th century. His work combined late Louis XVI and Empire designs and was characterised by the use of gilded caryatids on tables and chairs.

COUNTRY 1690–1850

This term is used to describe most simple furniture made between the late 17th and late 19th centuries, which combined both fashionable and more conservative features. As the name suggests, it was made by rural artisans, who modified more sophisticated designs to suit rural homes, but some was also made in cities. Pine and maple were the principal woods and surfaces were often painted, with very sparse decoration. Often, features of various styles were combined, those being chosen for ease of crafting. Thus turned William & Mary legs persisted long after they were no longer fashionable elsewhere, and cabriole legs are very rare. Windsor and slat back chairs are perhaps two of the most characteristic products of the Country style.

SHAKER FURNITURE 1790–1900

This furniture was made by the Shaker religious sect living in Massachusetts, New York and a few other states, and was in the finest tradition of country design. Its heyday lasted from 1820–70 and the furniture is characterised by its simplicity and utility. Form was subsidiary to function. Many pieces reflect the agricultural nature of the Shaker communities, such as tables for sorting seeds. Pine and maple were again the principal woods. Surfaces were unadorned and painted, legs were turned and slender.

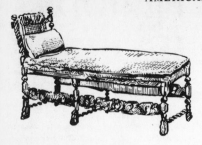

19TH CENTURY REVIVAL STYLES
GOTHIC REVIVAL 1840–1890

In its early stages the Gothic Revival was mainly expressed in decoration, with the use of details imitating historical ornament, such as quatrefoils, trefoils, tracery etc. Designs tended to be extravagant and florid and by the 1850s designers were turning rather towards Norman, Romanesque and Elizabethan models.

A further surge of neo-Gothicism came in the 1870s. This took a much simpler and functional form, and followed the purist theories of William Morris in trying to return to genuinely medieval designs. Walnut, oak and cherry were the woods most used, and decoration consisted of simple turned or cut out elements.

ROCOCO REVIVAL 1840–70

The Rococo Revival, also referred to at the time as the Louis XIV style, reached America around 1840 and persisted for about thirty years. It took a much bolder form than the 18th century style on which it was based, with ornament carved in very high relief on forms which were very 19th century in taste. Ornamentation consisted of florid roses, leaves, vines scrolls and shells, all richly carved on curving forms, with mahogany, rosewood and walnut as the preferred media. The main output of pieces in this style was concentrated in New York, Boston and Philadelphia, though there were makers all over the States. It was a style favored for 'Social' furniture, such as sofas, the newly introduced tête à têtes, center tables etc. The period too saw an increasing use of upholstery as techniques advanced and comfort became all important.

RENAISSANCE REVIVAL 1850–90

While it began as early as 1850, this is often looked on as a reaction to rococo. Features of both Renaissance and 18th century neoclassical style were combined on straight rectilinear forms. Porcelain and bronze plaques were often incorporated as embellishments, and popular motifs included flowers, medallions, classical busts, caryatids etc, combined with architecturally derived features such as pediments and columns. Light woods, such as walnut, were favored. Pieces were produced both by skilled craftsmen in New York, and mass produced in midwest factories, notably Grand Rapids.

EASTLAKE STYLE 1870–90

This was one of the styles conceived as a rejection of the flamboyance of most of the preceding 'revivals'. It was named for Charles Lock Eastlake, an influential English architect who advocated a return to simple, honest furniture, where there was a basic relationship between form and function.

17th century forms were recalled, and to avoid the simple repetition of classical motifs, new inspiration was sought for decoration from Middle Eastern and Far Eastern sources. Eastlake believed in letting the natural wood grain speak for itself and preferred oak, cherry and rosewood and walnut when not heavily varnished. Later, however, the movement fell away from his high standards, and a great deal of poor quality furniture was produced.

MISSION, AND ARTS & CRAFTS 1900–1925

These again were reactions against much of the design of the 19th century. The Mission style purported to be based on the furniture supposedly found in the old Franciscan Missions in California and was seen as a revival of medieval and other functional designs. It was, broadly speaking, the American expression of the British Arts & Crafts Movement.

Most pieces were executed in oak, forms were rectilinear and functional, the construction simple, often with obvious signs of handwork, such as exposed mortice and tenon joints. Chair backs consisted chiefly of flat vertical or horizontal splats. One of the most important proponents of the style was Gustav Stickley, who was uncompromising in the austerity of his pieces. His brothers, working in Grand Rapids, turned out pieces in a similar style, though they were more flexible in their approach to decoration.

EUROPEAN PERIODS

TUDOR 1485–1603
This term is used loosely to describe furniture which was emerging from the gothic period but which had not yet developed the characteristics of the Elizabethan period. It saw the introduction of new decorative motifs from the Continent, such as grotesque masks, caryatids and arabesques.

ELIZABETHAN 1558–1603
This, by definition, still comes into the Tudor period, but the style is characterised by even more florid decoration, such as strapwork, terminal figures, bulbous supports, festoons, swags, geometric and medallion panels, lozenges, arcading and pilasters.

INIGO JONES 1573–1652
English classical architect closely associated with the courts of James I and Charles I. He was one of the first Englishmen to study architecture in Italy and understand the rules of classicism. He was particularly influenced by Palladio and his style only became strongly influential in England in the 18th century when it was adopted by Lord Burlington and others.

JACOBEAN 1603–88
Strictly speaking the term should apply only to the reign of James I but the style continued long after his death. Oak is still the prime medium, with much use of marquetry or parquetry and poker work.

STUART 1603–1714
The later years of this period saw the introduction of walnut as a major medium alongside oak. The general rise in the standard of living at the time also led to the emergence of the cabinet maker as opposed to the humble joiner.

JEAN BÉRAIN 1639–1711
Bérain was official court designer to Louis XIV from 1674. His style features arabesques, singeries, fantastic figures, festoons, foliate ornament, birds etc. and he influenced styles in both Britain and the rest of Europe.

A C BOULLE 1642–1732
Born in 1642 in Paris, Boulle underwent a varied training and worked as a painter, architect, engraver and bronze worker as well as an ébeniste. He did not invent the marquetry now associated with his name, which was already in wide use in Italy, i.e. a combination of metal and tortoiseshell as an inlay, but he did evolve a particular type which he adapted to the taste and requirements of the time.

LOUIS XIV 1643–1715
Le Roi Soleil opened the Manufacture Royale des Meubles de la Couronne at Gobelins in 1642 to coordinate the control of all applied arts to the glorification of Crown and State. The principal innovations of the time were the chest of drawers or commode, and the bureau. This period also saw Boulle type furniture reach the height of its popularity.

GRINLING GIBBONS 1648–1721
Gibbons was an English wood carver and sculptor born in Rotterdam, who was patronised by Charles II and subsequent monarchs. He produced decorative carvings of flowers, swags of fruits etc in wood and sometimes stone for many Royal residences, and, most notably executed the choir stalls in St Paul's Cathedral.

CROMWELLIAN 1649–1660
This term is usually applied to English furniture of austere character made during the period of the Commonwealth or interregnum, but is also used loosely of related types.

CAROLEAN PERIOD 1660–1685
This saw a reaction against the austerity of the Puritan era which preceded it. The country was opened to a flood of Continental influences, all of which were characterised by their flamboyance and exuberance.

DANIEL MAROT 1661–1752
Marot was a French Protestant who fled to Holland after the revocation of the Edict of Nantes. He worked for William of Orange in a restrained baroque style and influenced several Dutch and English furniture and silver designers.

WILLIAM KENT 1685–1748
Kent was a versatile architect, landscape gardener and interior designer and was the most famous English exponent of Palladianism. His furniture and interiors showed a notable Baroque influence, however, with much elaborate gilt ornamentation and classical motifs carved out in softwoods or gesso.

WILLIAM & MARY 1689–1702
This period saw a general sobering of furniture styles, due to the staid influence of William's Dutch background. His great craftsman Daniel Marot, a Huguenot refugee, interpreted Louis XIV fashions in a quieter Dutch idiom.

EUROPEAN PERIODS

RÉGENCE STYLE 1700–20

Not to be confused with English Regency (the French Regency of Louis XV lasted from 1715–23) this is a French transitional style combining baroque and rococo elements. It is characterised by the increased use of veneer and marquetry, carving and gilding. Classical motifs from the Louis XIV era were also incorporated, such as acanthus leaves, C and S scrolls etc, but these were executed in a much lighter vein. Romantic, mythological subjects began to replace heroic ones, and oriental figures and those of the commedia dell' arte began to appear in decorations.

QUEEN ANNE 1702–1714

In this period walnut furniture reached its best phase. The emphasis was on graceful curves and a return to veneer instead of marquetry for decoration. Simple elegance was the hallmark of the period, demonstrated in such details as cabriole legs, hoop backed chairs and bracket feet.

GEORGIAN 1714–1820

The earlier Georgian period produced the heavier and more florid Baroque style, while the middle of the period saw the rise of such great designers as Hepplewhite, Chippendale and Sheraton. Mahogany competed with and finally supplanted walnut as the medium for the best quality pieces. The later period saw the Neo Classical Revival under Adam, with increasing use, too, of tropical woods.

THOMAS CHIPPENDALE 1715–1762

This English cabinet maker was famous for his elegant designs. His illustrated Collection of Rococo Furniture Designs which appeared in 1754 was the first comprehensive furniture catalogue and it was widely influential in Britain and America. It is his later, neo classical styles, however, which are generally considered to be his finest.

LOUIS XV 1723–1774

This period saw the popularisation of the rococo style, which introduced lightness and fantasy after the heaviness of the baroque period. A notable development of the period was Vernis Martin, the most celebrated process of lacquer imitation. At this time, too, oriental woods for marquetry and inlay began to be imported in quantity. The period saw the emergence of such items of furniture as the secrétaire à abattant and the bonheur du jour.

GEORGE HEPPLEWHITE 1727–1786

Hepplewhite was a celebrated furniture designer known for his neo-classical style. Basically he produced a simplified and more functional version of Adam designs. He worked mainly in inlaid mahogany or satinwood and his designs are characterised by straight, tapering legs and shield or oval chairbacks with openwork designs.

ADAM 1728–1792

Robert Adam (1728–92) was the son of the Palladian architect William Adam, who evolved a unique style combining rococo and neo classicism with the occasional use of gothic forms. He revived fine inlaid work, but in lighter colored woods. Chairs designed by him and his brother James were lighter, with straight legs tapering from square knee blocks to feet set in small plinths. The decoration of his mature period was delicate, with widely spaced ornamental features joined by festoons and swags.

ANGELICA KAUFFMAN (1741–1807)

Kauffman was a Swiss painter who divided her career between London and Rome. She was employed on decorative work in country houses designed by the Adam Brothers, painting, for example, decorative tops for their dainty tables.

THOMAS SHERATON 1751–1806

Sheraton made his name with the publication of his Cabinet Maker's and Upholsterer's Drawing Book 1791–94. He was influenced by Adam and French styles and advocated light and delicate furniture characterised by straight lines, often accentuated by reeding or fluting, and inlaid decoration. He had a particular fondness for fruitwood. Handles are typically circular.

LOUIS XVI 1774–1793

This period saw a return to classical styles after the exuberance of rococo. At this time many decorative processes were finally perfected, such as ormolu, marquetry etc. and an innovation was the use of porcelain to embellish furniture.

THOMAS SHEARER circa 1780

Shearer was an 18th century contemporary of Hepplewhite and Sheraton who influenced many American cabinet makers between 1790–1810. He is noted in particular for his washstands and dressing tables with ingenious fittings. Much of his work has been credited to his more prominent contemporaries, though in fact it was they who stole many a leaf out of Shearer's book.

DIRECTOIRE STYLE 1790–1804

This is a transitional style which combined the elements of Louis XVI and Empire styles and was popular between 1790 and 1804. It was characterised by simple, clean lines, and neo-classical forms and ornamentation were still favored. In France, revolutionary symbols, such as tricolor rosettes were sometimes used, while American Directoire similarly featured on occasion indigenous ornamentation. Towards the end of the period, Egyptian themes became popular, following Napoleon's Egyptian campaign.

EUROPEAN PERIODS

REGENCY 1800–1830

Strictly speaking this period applies only to the Regency of George, Prince of Wales from 1811–1820, although it is more generally used to cover the period between 1800 and the accession of William IV in 1830. During this time, dark exotic woods and veneers were popular, set off by ormolu mounts and grilles for doors. A vogue for furniture purporting to be based on classical models ran concurrently with a fondness for chinoiserie and oriental motifs, and some fine lacquer work was produced. Initially elegant, the style later became somewhat clumsy.

EMPIRE 1804–1815

This period represents the basically neo classical style in decorative arts which developed during the Napoleonic Empire, and it coincided with the contemporary interest in archaeology. Dark woods, such as rosewood, were popular, sparsely ornamented with ormolu. Shapes tended to be plain, but caryatids were often used as supports.

BEIDERMEIER 1815–60

This was a German-based decorative style conceived as a reaction against the ornate designs of the 18th century. Early pieces were rectilinear and simple though the use of curves became more widespread in chair backs and legs in the middle period. Scroll forms and animal heads became popular after 1840. Dark mahogany, ash, birch and cherry were favored woods, and the style is associated with comfort rather than display. There was much use of horsehair padding and velvet upholstery, and the style is associated with the emergent bourgeoisie.

VICTORIAN 1837–1901

During the early Victorian period, British furniture design reached its nadir. The emphasis was on rich and elaborate carving, and there was much use of the substitute materials which new technology was making available. Of these, the only one of any real quality was papier mâché. After 1851, the style became more uniform, characterised by the use of solid wood, more severe outlines, and though carving remained as a principal form of embellishment, it was more constrained and carefully disposed. The late Victorian period saw a gothic revival, under Pugin and Burges, and the revolt of William Morris and others led to the development of the Arts & Crafts Movement.

ARTS & CRAFTS

This artistic movement originated in late 19th century England round the central figure of William Morris, who urged a return to medieval standards of craftsmanship in the face of industrialisation and mass production. Its influence extended into many fields such as furniture, ceramics, silver and textiles. Early furniture was simple and solid in construction, the natural beauty of the wood being used for decorative effect. Oak, elm, walnut and sometimes acacia were the favored woods.

The movement continued into the 20th century, though some earlier doctrines, such as the rejection of the machine, were later called into question.

ART NOUVEAU

This decorative style of the 19th and 20th centuries in Europe and America is generally regarded as having reached its peak with the Paris Exhibition of 1900. It drew heavily on natural forms for decorative inspiration, and was distinguished by the frequent use of flowing, plant-like motifs, often extended and convoluted, in conjunction with elements of fantasy and eroticism.

JUGENDSTIL

This is the general name for Austrian and German design in the Art Nouveau manner. It was named after the magazine 'Jugend' published in Munich from 1896 and found expression in the works of the Munich School. They incorporated neo-rococo elements of French Art Nouveau in the form of stylised flowers and figures and languid, trailing lines. Later the style became more geometric, influenced among others by Charles Rennie Mackintosh.

EDWARDIAN 1901–1910

Under the influence of Art Nouveau and the Arts and Crafts Movement, Edwardian furniture styles brightened up considerably after the darker excesses of High Victoriana. Lighter woods became popular, and the period was characterised by a lightness and daintiness of design, with much use of attractive inlays.

ART DECO

This European style emerged from about 1910 and lasted until the mid 1930s. Until about 1928, stylised roses and other plant forms constituted the most popular motifs, superseded thereafter by Cubist inspired decoration. The emphasis became very much on geometric, angular designs and simple, bold forms with a correspondingly bold use of bright colors.

MONARCHS

HENRY IV	1399 – 1413	COMMONWEALTH	1649 – 1660
HENRY V	1413 – 1422	CHARLES II	1660 – 1685
HENRY VI	1422 – 1461	JAMES II	1685 – 1689
EDWARD IV	1461 – 1483	WILLIAM & MARY	1689 – 1695
EDWARD V	1483 – 1483	WILLIAM III	1695 – 1702
RICHARD III	1483 – 1485	ANNE	1702 – 1714
HENRY VII	1485 – 1509	GEORGE I	1714 – 1727
HENRY VIII	1509 – 1547	GEORGE II	1727 – 1760
EDWARD VI	1547 – 1553	GEORGE III	1760 – 1820
MARY	1553 – 1558	GEORGE IV	1820 – 1830
ELIZABETH	1558 – 1603	WILLIAM IV	1830 – 1837
JAMES I	1603 – 1625	VICTORIA	1837 – 1901
CHARLES I	1625 – 1649	EDWARD VII	1901 – 1910

CHINESE DYNASTIES

Shang	1766 – 1123BC	5 Dynasties	907 – 960
Zhou	1122 – 249BC	Liao	907 – 1125
Warring States	403 – 221BC	Song	960 – 1279
Qin	221 – 207BC	Jin	1115 – 1234
Han	206BC – AD220	Yuan	1260 – 1368
6 Dynasties	317 – 589	Ming	1368 – 1644
Sui	590 – 618	Qing	1644 – 1911
Tang	618 – 906		

REIGN PERIODS

MING

Hongwu	1368 – 1398	Hongzhi	1488 – 1505
Jianwen	1399 – 1402	Zhengde	1506 – 1521
Yongle	1403 – 1424	Jiajing	1522 – 1566
Hongxi	1425	Longqing	1567 – 1572
Xuande	1426 – 1435	Wanli	1573 – 1620
Zhengtong	1436 – 1449	Taichang	1620
Jingtai	1450 – 1456	Tianqi	1621 – 1627
Tianshun	1457 – 1464	Chongzheng	1628 – 1644
Chenghua	1465 – 1487		

QING

Shunzhi	1644 – 1662	Daoguang	1821 – 1850
Kangxi	1662 – 1722	Xianfeng	1851 – 1861
Yongzheng	1723 – 1735	Tongzhi	1862 – 1874
Qianlong	1736 – 1795	Guangxu	1875 – 1908
Jiali	1796 – 1820	Xuantong	1908 – 1911

HANDLES

| 1550
Tudor
drop | 1560
Early
Stuart
loop | 1570
Early
Stuart
loop | 1620
Early
Stuart
loop | 1660
Stuart
drop | 1680
Stuart
drop |

| 1690
William &
Mary solid
backplate | 1700
William &
Mary split
tail | 1700
Queen Anne
solid back | 1705
Queen Anne
ring | 1710
Queen Anne
loop | 1720
Early
Georgian
pierced |

| 1720
Early
Georgian
brass drop | 1730
Cut away
backplate | 1740
Georgian
plain brass
loop | 1750
Georgian
shield drop | 1755
French
style | 1760
Rococo
style |

| 1765
Chinese
style | 1770
Georgian
ring | 1780
Late Georgian
stamped | 1790
Late Georgian
stamped | 1810
Regency
knob | 1820
Regency
lions mask |

| 1825
Campaign | 1840
Early
Victorian
porcelain | 1850
Victorian
reeded | 1880
Porcelain or
wood knob | 1890
Late Victorian
loop | 1910
Art
Nouveau |

CHAIR BACKS

1660
Charles II

1705
Queen Anne

1745
Chippendale

1745
Chippendale

1750
Georgian

1750
Hepplewhite

1750
Chippendale

1760
French Rococo

1760
Gothic

1760
Splat back

1770
Chippendale
ladder back

1785
Windsor
wheel back

1785
Lancashire
spindle back

1785
Lancashire
ladder back

1790
Shield and
feathers

1795
Shield back

1795
Hepplewhite

1795
Hepplewhite
camel back

1795
Hepplewhite

1810
Late Georgian
bar back

CHAIR BACKS

1810
Thomas Hope
'X' frame

1810
Regency
rope back

1815
Regency

1815
Regency
cane back

1820
Regency

1820
Empire

1820
Regency
bar back

1825
Regency
bar back

1830
Regency
bar back

1830
bar back

1830
William IV
bar back

1830
William IV

1835
Lath back

1840
Victorian
balloon back

1845
Victorian

1845
Victorian
bar back

1850
Victorian

1860
Victorian

1870
Victorian

1875
Cane back

LEGS

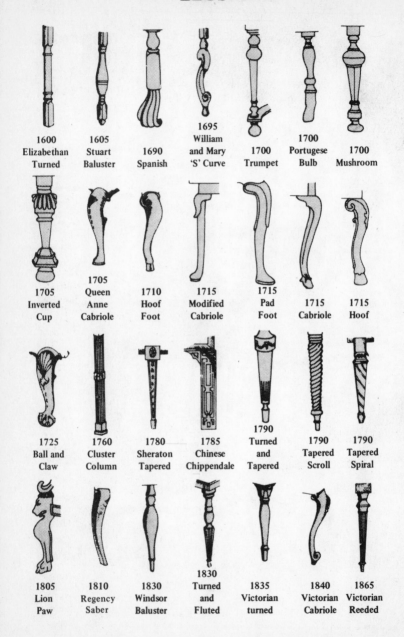

1600
Elizabethan
Turned

1605
Stuart
Baluster

1690
Spanish

1695
William
and Mary
'S' Curve

1700
Trumpet

1700
Portugese
Bulb

1700
Mushroom

1705
Inverted
Cup

1705
Queen
Anne
Cabriole

1710
Hoof
Foot

1715
Modified
Cabriole

1715
Pad
Foot

1715
Cabriole

1715
Hoof

1725
Ball and
Claw

1760
Cluster
Column

1780
Sheraton
Tapered

1785
Chinese
Chippendale

1790
Turned
and
Tapered

1790
Tapered
Scroll

1790
Tapered
Spiral

1805
Lion
Paw

1810
Regency
Saber

1830
Windsor
Baluster

1830
Turned
and
Fluted

1835
Victorian
turned

1840
Victorian
Cabriole

1865
Victorian
Reeded

FEET

1690
Wooden
Wheel

1690
Ball

1700
Bracket

1700
Spanish

1710
Hoof

1715
Pad

1725
Ball and
Claw

1735
Cabriole
Leg Foot

1740
Stylized
Hoof

1740
Ogee

1745
French
Knurl

1750
Dolphin

1750
English
Knurl

1755
Elaborate
bracket

1760
Splay

1760
Gutta
Foot

1770
Tapered
socket

1775
Peg and
Plate

1790
Spiral
Twist

1790
Wheel
Castor

1790
Spade

1800
Fluted
Ball

1805
Decorative
Socket

1805
Paw

1805
Regency

1810
Socket

1815
Lion Paw

1830
Regency

1830
Victorian
Scroll

1860
Victorian
Bun

Fine Italian agate cameo, 1in. high, late 16th century.

Solid agate silver shaped sauceboat.

George III circular gold mounted gray agate toilet box and cover, circa 1800, 5in. high.

Early 20th century Austrian or Hungarian agate bon bon dish with gem-set mounts, 9.1cm. diam.

German agate standing salt, circa 1600, 8½in. high.

Staffordshire solid agate pecten-shell teapot and cover, 7¼in. wide.

Late 19th century Russian figure of a collie carved from milky gray agate, 6.4cm. high.

Solid agate cream jug, 4in. high, circa 1750.

Late 19th century alabaster figure of an eagle, by W. Gebler, 17½in. high.

Coloured alabaster bust of a young woman in a square necked dress, circa 1890, 14½in. tall.

Nottingham alabaster relief of the Assumption of the Virgin, early 15th century, 16in. high.

Early 17th century English kneeling alabaster figure, 20in. high.

Large Egyptian alabaster jar, early Dynastic period, 11½in. high.

Italian alabaster group, 1880-1900, 27½in. high.

Gilt bronze and alabaster figure entitled 'Nature unveiling herself', circa 1893, 42in. high.

Alabaster jar of Necho II, barrel-shaped with twin handles, 13¼in. high, circa 610-595 B.C.

Zodiac fortune teller, coin-operated machine, circa 1940, 24½in. high.

American 'Twenty-one' gambling machine in cast alloy and oak casing, circa 1930, 13½in. wide.

English 'Pussy Shooter' amusement machine with glazed window, circa 1935, 76in. high.

Auto-stereoscope in oak casing with viewer and coin slot at top, circa 1930, 22½in. high.

Mutoscope by the International Mutoscope Reel Co., circa 1905, 74in. high.

Early Rowland Pier Head amusement machine 'The Racer', circa 1900, 19in. wide.

Allwin De Luxe amusement machine in oak case with glazed front, 27in. high, circa 1935.

'Laughing Sailor' amusement machine bearing Ruffler & Walker plaque, circa 1935, 68½in. high.

ANIMALIA

Very rare passenger pigeon, mounted on branch, 22in. high, in glass dome.

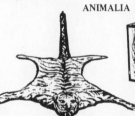

A large tiger-skin 9ft.8ins. long.

Cased stuffed fish, labelled 'Thames Trout', dated 1883.

Stuffed barn owl.

A large stuffed moose head.

Stuffed and mounted pelican in glass fronted case, 2ft. 7in. high.

An Indian long-haired black mountain bear.

Huge mounted head of an Indian water buffalo.

Pair of well articulated upper arm defences from the 17th century.

19th century sheet iron articulated helmet of Cromwellian design, circa 1830, 14in. high.

An Allemaine collar of the 16th century from a suit of armor.

Scarce 18th or 19th century Japanese russet face-guard mempo in red and black lacquer.

A 17th century Cromwellian trooper's helmet, skull formed in two pieces.

19th century Japanese suit of armor.

An Indo-Persian suit of chain mail, 16/17th century.

Italian 17th century suit of horseman's armor with close helmet.

AUTOMATONS

Musical piggy duo automaton, 1ft.3in. high, French.

Dancing negress automaton with key wound mechanism, in good condition, 10½in. high.

A levitation automaton depicting Snow White lying on a couch, 45in. x 38in., circa 1920.

Late 19th century French musical rabbit automaton, 9in. high.

Late 19th century French musical automaton, 'The Hunter at Rest', 2ft.3in.

Large French singing bird automaton, 18½in. high, circa 1900.

Late 19th century French musical seascape automaton, 1ft.8in. high.

19th century clown with dancing midget, musical box inside.

Mother-of-pearl inlaid rosewood barometer, circa 1850, 44¾in. high.

Inlaid mahogany stick barometer by Negretti, 1850, 44in. long.

Louis XV barometer in boulle case.

George II walnut stick barometer with arched portico cresting and ribbed bowed base, 42in. high.

Victorian oak cased barometer.

A circular barometer in brass case on ebonized stand.

Late 19th century combined clock, thermometer, barometer and barograph, 2ft.3in. wide.

Victorian wall barometer in an oak case.

A small 19th century timepiece and barometer in brass horseshoe pattern case, 6in. wide.

Oak barometer and timepiece, 1880's, 44in. high.

Early 18th century walnut pillar barometer, 3ft.3in. high.

Unusual Dutch walnut barometer, mid 18th century, 3ft.11in. high.

Very rare George II column barometer, 2ft.11in. high.

Mahogany wheel barometer in the form of a longcase clock, by J. Hallifax, Barnsley, 45in. high.

BRONZE

Stylish WMF polished bronze stemmed dish, circa 1910, 19cm. high.

Large Art Deco spelter group, 32in. wide, Paris.

Heyner bronze letter opener, 30cm. long, circa 1900.

Mid 19th century bronze group of Una and the Lion, signed G. Geefs, 43.2cm. high.

Bronze figure of Perseus arming by Sir Alfred Gilbert, 1880's, 14¼in. high.

19th century bronze figure of an old man, 9in. long.

Late 19th century bronze by W. Szczblewski.

One of a pair of Komai style bronze vases, 17½in. high.

Bronze and ivory figure by H. Chiparus Etling, Paris, circa 1920, 7¾in. high.

Early 20th century bronze group signed T. Campaiola, 24in. high.

Late Ming dynasty bronze figure, 11¾in. high.

Bronze figure of Icarus, by Alfred Gilbert, 48.5cm. high.

'Salammbô', a gilt bronze bust cast from a design by Louis Moreau, of a young female with long flowing hair, 74.5cm. high.

Good Philippe bronze and ivory group, 1920's, 48cm. high.

Bronze and ivory Art Deco figure.

Mid 19th century bronze group by Charles Cumberworth, 13½in. high.

Bronze and ivory figure of 'The Sunworshipper' by Preiss, 1930's, 18.5cm. high.

Bronze figure of a jaguar, 22¼in. long, 1920's.

Bronze figure of a grazing ewe, by Rosa Bonheur, circa 1860, 6in. wide.

Gilt bronze group of a Bobsleigh team, circa 1936, 28.5cm. high.

Large Egyptian bronze statue of a cat.

Early 16th century Paduan bronze group of a female satyr and her child, 7¼in. high.

Art Deco metal figure by Rischmann, 22¾in. high.

13th century Pagan figure of the Buddha in bronze, 10¾in. high.

Bronze group of a centaur attacking a warrior, 21in. high.

American bronze figure, signed Paul Herzel, circa 1910.

19th century Japanese bronze, 4ft.4in. long.

Bronze figure of a horse, circa 1880, 6in. wide.

19th century Japanese bronze figure of a Samurai warrior, 10in. high.

Bronze figure of a tribesman, 41cm. high.

A pair of bronze horses, 14½in. high, circa 1900.

Spelter lampstand, after Bouret, circa 1890, 28in. high.

Gilt bronze group of three putti, 1850's, 10¾in. wide.

Early 17th century Florentine bronze figure from the Susini workshop, 6¾in. high.

19th century Japanese bronze group.

Mid 17th century oval bronze relief by Daniel Neuberger, 12¾in. long.

Chiparus bronze and ivory figure of a dancing girl, 43.5cm. high, 1920's.

Franz Bergmann cold-painted bronze figure, circa 1910, 5in. high.

Bronze figure of David, circa 1880, 29in. high, signed F. Barbedienne.

French bronze bulldog on a square base, 11in. long, signed P. Dinby, circa 1900.

Modern bronze bust of an Indian, 14in. high.

19th century bronze cavalry charger and trooper by J. Willis Good.

Late 17th century Flemish bronze mortar and T-shaped pestle, 5½in. high.

Spelter figure of a girl on an onyx and marble base, circa 1920, 1ft. 6in. long.

Bronze group of two dogs, circa 1880, 9in. long, signed Lalouette.

15th century bronze bust of the Buddha by Sukh'o'tai, 28½in. high.

Early 16th century Paduan equestrian group, 16¾in. high.

Elaborate bronze figure of an Egyptian priestess.

Late 19th century bronze lion, signed Barye.

Hagenauer bronze vase, circa 1910, 11.5cm. high.

Stylish Guigner Art Deco gilt-bronze group, 54.75cm high, 1930's.

Early 17th century Venetian bronze door knocker, 16in. high.

Fine bronze of a Red Indian by Carl Kauba, on marble plinth, 19th century, 16in. high.

Small Egyptian bronze, 10in. high, circa 1090 B.C.

Bronze lion cast in the T'ang style, 10in. long.

Stylish bronze figure of a vulture, 20cm. high, 1920's.

A bronze cow with raised head, signed I. Bonheur, circa 1870, 6¼in. high.

Preiss bronze and ivory figure of a schoolboy, 21cm. high.

Bronze group by Isadore Bonheur, 20¼in. wide.

20th century Italian bronze figure of a fawn, 34¼in. high.

Untypical ivory and bronze figure by Franz Preiss.

17th/18th century Italian bronze figure of Christ, 9½in. high.

19th century French bronze group signed L. Longepied, 19in. high.

Splashed gilt bronze vase, Chinese, 18th century, 29.5cm. high.

George III oval satin-wood tea caddy with hinged lid, 6in. wide.

Victorian coromandel wood games compendium in box, 13½in. wide.

One of a pair of George III canta-loup shaped tea caddies, 4½in. wide.

Mid 19th century French gilt metal jewel casket with five porcelain panels, 20.5cm. long.

One of a pair of George III mahogany and satin-wood knife boxes, 22.5cm. wide.

Mahogany 'Duke of York' apothecary cabinet, circa 1780.

Coachbuilder's tool chest and contents, tools bearing the stamp of J. Hartley, circa 1839.

One of a pair of mahogany cutlery vases in George III style, 28in. high.

Lacquered work box with lift-up lid and four drawers.

Mid 19th century artist's paintbox, 1ft.10in. wide, English.

English box and counters, 1755-1760, enameled on copper, 6.5cm. wide.

Late 19th century oak cased calendar.

Victorian coromandel-wood box by Baxter, London, 1856, 8½in. wide.

Mid 17th century oak spice cabinet, 15in. wide.

Mahogany and inlaid decanter box with four cut-glass decan-ters, 8½in. high.

Georgian satinwood in-laid tea caddy.

Small, Victorian tooled leather stationery box with fitted interior.

Stobwasser box painted with La Toilette.

Early 19th century covered oval quill work box with ivory finial, 5½in. long.

Late 19th century Indian ivory and ebony box.

An excellent quality late 18th century tea caddy with rolled paper decoration, 5in. high.

Crocodile skin traveling dressing case with gold mounted fittings.

Tunbridgeware coromandel box by Thos. Barton, circa 1870, 9½in. wide.

Late 18th century octagonal lacquer Kojubako, signed Zohiko.

19th century Japanese Suzuribako with fitted tray.

Table square spice box with named sectioned interior, circa 1840.

One of a set of six English mid 19th century tobacco containers, 1ft.5in.

George III woodworker's tool chest in a pine case, 3ft.6in. wide.

Oak candle box, circa 1790, 13in. wide.

19th century English lacquer box by Jennens and Bettridge.

Regency mother-of-pearl inlaid tortoiseshell veneered tea caddy, circa 1820, 6¾in. wide.

Edwardian C.W.S. biscuit tin.

Tortoiseshell and mother-of-pearl inlaid tea caddy.

Gilt metal jewel casket with pierced hinged lid and sides, 1880's, 16.5cm. long.

'Intarsia' brass mounted and inlaid wood casket, circa 1900, 14cm. long.

George III ivory veneered tea caddy of oval shape, lid with pineapple finial, circa 1790.

19th century lacquer Suzuribako, 9¼in. wide.

Oak decanter box by H. H. Dobson & Sons, London, circa 1850, 9¾in. long.

19th century mahogany domestic medicine chest with rising top, 30cm. high.

Burr-satin birch scent box, containing four scent bottles and stoppers, circa 1850, 5½in. wide.

One of a pair of George III mahogany knife boxes, circa 1780, 8¾in. high.

Unusual 19th century Chinese black lacquer tea caddy.

Canteen of Old English pattern table cutlery by Martin Hall & Co., Sheffield, in oak case.

18th century oak candle box with sliding front, 16in. high.

George III ivory and pewter tea caddy, 5in. high.

Commonwealth carved oak bible box, 1657, 2ft. wide.

Mid 19th century Tunbridge-ware coromandel box by Thos. Barton, enclosing three graduated drawers, 8in. wide.

Tortoiseshell tea caddy with engraved plate on front.

Regency penwork tea caddy, 9in. wide.

Mid 19th century tortoiseshell and silvered metal mounted box.

17th century French red leather casket, 16in. long.

Circular pollard wood snuff box, circa 1820, 8.2cm. diameter.

Reco Capey carved ebony box and cover, 21cm. high.

Victorian satinwood square shaped tea caddy, 11cm. wide.

Rosewood and satinwood portable writing box, circa 1900, 12in. wide.

19th century mahogany and brass coal box.

Adjustable Tunbridgeware bookshelf with two arched ends, circa 1870, 11½in. wide, closed.

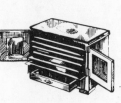

Walnut and marquetry humidor, circa 1880, 14 x 19½in.

Unusual carved oak offertory box with iron lock and chain.

Early 19th century tortoiseshell tea caddy, inlaid with mother-of-pearl.

Late 18th century George III cutlery urn of ovoid form in mahogany with boxwood and ebony lines, 27in. high.

Victorian Tunbridgeware stamp box.

Rare George II japanned tea caddy, circa 1740, 10¼in. wide.

Late Victorian pine specimen chest.

CAMERAS

Fine quarter-plate field camera by Sanderson.

Japanese Canon Model 7 35mm. camera and filter, in leather case, circa 1962.

Rare Johnson pantoscopic camera, circa 1860.

'The Telephot' ferro-type button camera, circa 1900, English.

Stirn's small waistcoat detective camera, in brass, second model, circa 1888.

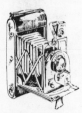

Newman & Guardia New Ideal Sibyl folding camera, circa 1925.

J. Lancaster half-plate 'instantograph' collapsible camera, circa 1905.

Ensign tropical roll-film reflex camera, circa 1925.

CANE HANDLES

French Art Nouveau cane handle, circa 1900.

English ivory handled walking stick, circa 1830.

Walking stick with wood shaft and handle and horn ferrule, circa 1900, 88.4cm. long.

Late 19th century Meissen parasol handle, 4.3cm. high.

18th century ivory and Narwhal walking stick, 96.5cm. long.

Rhinoceros horn and silver pique cane handle, circa 1700, 12.5cm. long.

Late 19th century malacca walking cane with scrimshaw ball grip set with a compass, 81.5cm. long.

German porcelain cane handle, 2½in. high, late 18th century.

English ivory pique cane handle, 4in. high, 1667.

Early 19th century Italian parcel gilt cane handle, 9.5cm. long.

Carved oak sternboard from the boat of an 18th century Dutch flagship, 33in. wide.

Mid 18th century South German carved wood group.

Early 18th century English fruitwood relief of two cherub heads flanking a chalice, 30cm. high.

Early 17th century yew wood mortar, 6¼in. high.

Balsa wood mask made for the 'Goelede' society, Yoruba tribe.

Late 17th century figure of Putai, in lacquered wood, 22in. high.

19th century American wooden butter stamp with incised deer, 4in. diam.

Lower Rhine oak relief, 19½in. high, circa 1500.

Maori carved wooden house post, before 1840, 4ft.2½in. high.

Large Egyptian wood mummy mask.

19th century Scandinavian painted bride's box of plywood strips, 17½in. long.

Bas relief wood sculpture, by Norman Forrest, 1930's, 93cm. high.

17th century Spanish carved wood and painted polychrome religious group, 19in.

Carved walnut figure group of two cavaliers, 41in. high.

One of a pair of early George III rococo giltwood wall brackets, circa 1750, 1ft.wide.

Atelier Hagenauer patinated metal and carved wood head, 27cm. high, circa 1920.

A pair of carved walnut candlesticks, circa 1900, 18in. high.

19th century Dutch cart-front decorated in poly-chrome.

Fine mid 19th century Italian ship's figurehead from The Benvolio.

Maori carved wood present box, 5½in. long.

Fine carved cartouche in the manner of Matthias Locke.

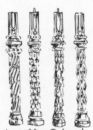

A set of four Tudor oak colonnettes, early 16th century, 25in. high.

17th century Flemish boxwood relief of Adam and Eve in the Garden of Eden, 14.5cm. wide.

Large 18th century lignum vitae cup, 19in. high.

Hawaiian wooden image, 10¼in. high.

19th century Swiss bear furniture.

Wood sculpture on slate base, 1930's, 93cm. high.

Fine 14th century French walnut group of the Virgin and Child, 42.5cm. high.

Lower Rhine relief in oak, 19½in. high, circa 1500.

Pair of middle Rhine late Gothic oak figures, 35in. high, circa 1480.

Pair of Elizabethan box-wood nutcrackers, 1583, 4½in. high.

Mid 17th century Dutch or German maplewood spoon, 17.5cm. long.

19th century Scandinavian carved and painted butter tub with flat cover, 13in. diam.

Late Ptolemaic mask, 1st century B.C.

Carved walnut hunting plaque, circa 1870, 47in. high, Swiss.

Fruitwood watch stand, 230mm. high.

15th century North Italian polychrome oak group of St. Christopher and a child, 25½in. high.

Finely carved pinewood cockerel, circa 1820, 18in. diameter.

Turned wood apothecary's jar, late 18th century, 9½in. high.

18th century Norwegian polychrome beechwood Skala, 9in. high.

19th century Japanese carved, gessoed and painted Oriental deity, 29½in. high.

Carved and painted wooden mask from West Africa.

18th century pair of Dutch dummy board figures, 45in. high.

Rowley Gallery giltwood low relief, circa 1925, 71cm. high.

American pine candle box with carved decoration on all sides, 9¾in. long.

Early 19th century tobacconist's sign of a Highlander.

Painted wood picture frame, circa 1900, 40½in. wide.

Elm bellows with brass center decoration piece, 25in. long, circa 1790.

CAR MASCOTS

Old Bill by Bruce Bairnsfather.

Red Ashay glass car mascot in the form of a woman's head, 23cm. wide, 1930's.

Lalique glass dragon-fly car mascot, 20.5cm. long, 1920's, signed.

Telco Pup car mascot.

Lalique cockerels head.

Kingfisher enameled mascot.

A standing figure of the Esso man, 5½in. high.

Nickel plated Minerva mascot.

Lalique glass hawk mascot, engraved, 1920's, 16.5cm. high.

Brass Astor car mascot.

CHANDELIERS

Georgian gilt metal mounted cut-glass twelve-light chandelier, 43in. high.

Gilt bronze and Favrile glass ceiling fixture by Tiffany, 17in. high.

18th century English cast brass chandelier of six arms, 17in. high.

George II giltwood chandelier of fifteen lights, circa 1750, by Matthias Locke.

Edwardian gilt bronze and glass chandelier in late 18th century style, fitted for electricity.

One of a pair of cast iron gas chandeliers, circa 1870, 77in. high.

Rare William IV gilt brass colzaoil lantern of six lights, circa 1830, 2ft.1in. diam.

Iridescent Favrile glass chandelier by Tiffany, shade 14in. high.

ALBARELLO

Dated Tuscan albarello, 13.3cm. high, 1600.

Late 15th/early 16th century Sicilian albarello, 31cm. high.

Venetian albarello of dumb bell shape, 1578, 14.2cm. high.

A Sicilian albarello, 20cm. high, 17th century.

ANSBACH

Ansbach two-handled seau crenelle with gilt dentil rim, circa 1770, 17.5cm. wide.

18th century Ansbach faience tankard, with pewter footrim, 1791, 24.5cm. high.

Ansbach shaped circular plate with Ozier rim, circa 1775, 23cm. diam.

One of a pair of Ansbach equestrian figures, circa 1730, 24.5cm. high.

AUSTRIAN

Late 19th century Austrian porcelain plaque, in brass frame, 10in. high.

Austrian glazed earthenware vase, circa 1910, 20.5cm. high.

Austrian pottery figure of a young boy, in the manner of Michael Powolny, 31.5cm. high.

An Austrian glazed earthenware jardiniere and stand, circa 1905.

BAYREUTH

Bayreuth Hausmaler teabowl and saucer, circa 1740.

Fine and rare Bayreuth Hausmaler bowl, 18.5cm. diam., circa 1740.

Royal Bayreuth sunbonnet baby's hair receiver, Germany, circa 1900, 2¾in. diam.

Royal Bayreuth figural milk jug in the form of an eagle, circa 1900, 6¼in. high.

BELLARMINE

Antique brown glazed stoneware bellarmine jug, 13in. high.

Early 17th century Frenchen stoneware bellarmine jug, 25cm. high.

Late 16th/early 17th century bellarmine jug, slightly damaged.

Small 17th century tiger-ware bellarmine bottle with gray beard mask and circular seal, 8½in. high.

BELLEEK

Early Belleek basket with lattice work side and a handle of entwined branches, 11in. wide.

Belleek tea kettle on stand.

Belleek croaking frog, circa 1900, 5½in. high.

Belleek honeypot in the form of a beehive, 6¼in. high.

BERLIN

19th century Berlin plaque of the Virgin and Child.

Mid 18th century Berlin pewter mounted faience tankard, with portrait of Frederick the Great, 23.5cm. high.

One of a pair of Berlin porcelain cabinet cups and saucers with gilt decoration.

One of a pair of Berlin covered chocolate pots, 7¾in. and 5½in. high, circa 1830.

BLUE & WHITE

Late 19th century blue and white dish with foliate scroll border, 54.7cm. diam.

Late 19th century blue and white vase.

Blue and white lavatory pan, 'Niagara'.

One of a pair of late 19th century blue and white vases and covers, 46.5cm. high.

BOTTGER

Rare Augsburg decorated Bottger pagoda figure, circa 1720, 8.3cm. high.

BOULOGNE

Boulogne crackle glazed pottery figure, 61cm. high, 1920's.

BOW

One of a pair of rare Bow wall pockets, 8¼in. long, about 1770.

BRISTOL

Bristol made cider mug, 1842, 5in. high.

Rare Bottger/early Meissen teapot and cover, 11cm. high, circa 1730.

Boulogne glazed pottery figure, 47.5cm. high, 1925.

Pair of Bow figures of a gallant and lady, 6in. high, about 1760.

One of a pair of Bristol pearlware documentary spirit barrels, 1834, 12cm. high.

Rare Bottger double-handled beaker and saucer, circa 1720-25.

BOW

Bow blue and white cider jug, circa 1754, 8¼in. high.

Bow plate in Chelsea style, circa 1760, 23cm. diam.

Fine Bristol teapot and cover, 6in. high, about 1775.

Very rare Bottger jug and cover, circa 1720.

Ormolu mounted Bow figure of a girl flanked by bull-rushes, circa 1765, 21.5cm. high.

Bow triple shell salt, 18cm. wide, circa 1760, slightly restored.

Rare Bristol figure of a goatherder, 10¾in. high, about 1775.

BRITISH

Victorian pottery butter dish.

Victorian brown glazed pottery cheese dish.

Late Victorian pottery 'Quick Cooker'.

Goat cream jug, circa 1910, 5½in. high, in very good condition.

Parian bust of Queen Victoria, signed Noble, 2ft. high.

Victorian jug and basin set.

Stoneware ginger beer bottle.

English porcelain figure of the Duke of Wellington, circa 1800, 29cm. high.

BURMANTOFT

Burmantoft vase, about 1885, painted by 'L.K', 8½in. high.

Burmantoft jardiniere and stand, 50½in. high.

Burmantoft dish, circa 1885, 16in. diam.

Burmantoft vase, about 1885, painted by 'L. K.', 9¾in. high.

CAPODIMONTE

Capodimonte circular sugar bowl and cover, circa 1758, 10.5cm. diam.

Capodimonte (Carlo III) figure of a Callot dwarf in peaked hat, circa 1750, 8cm. high.

Large Capodimonte porcelain table lamp with four dancing figures on base.

Extremely rare Capodimonte Commedia Dell'Arte group of the Harlequin and two other figures, by Guiseppe Gricci, dated around 1750.

CARDEW

Michael Cardew Wenford Bridge stoneware stool, 1970's, 30.8cm. diam.

A Michael Cardew Winchcombe pottery vase, the ovoid body with pronounced potting lines, 32cm. high.

Michael Cardew large slipware dish, circa 1930, 16½in. diam.

A Michael Cardew Abuja stoneware wine jar and cover, 31.5cm. high, circa 1959.

CASTEL DURANTE

Castel Durante dated wet drug jar, 1644, 22.5cm. high.

Late 16th century Castel Durante drug jar with strap handle, 21cm. high.

Mid 17th century Castel Durante bottle, 22.5cm. high.

Rare documentary Castel Durante drug jar, 35cm. high, 1562.

CASTELLI

Late 18th century Castelli plaque, 26.8cm. long.

Early 18th century Castelli plate decorated with Fortitude sitting on a tomb, 19cm. diam.

18th century Castelli maijolica plaque.

Late 17th/early 18th century Castelli plaque of circular shape, 26cm. diam.

CAUGHLEY

A Caughley cylindrical mug printed in blue, 6in. high, circa 1780.

Part of a Caughley part tea and coffee service of thirty-two pieces, painted in gray black and gilt.

Caughley teabowl and saucer painted in underglaze blue, circa 1785.

Miniature Caughley coffee pot in underglaze blue, 3½in. high.

CHINA

CHALKWARE

Mid 19th century chalkware rooster, Pennsylvania, 11 in. high.

Mid 19th century chalkware sitting dog, Pennsylvania, 13¼ in. high.

CHAMPIONS BRISTOL

Fine Champions Bristol bell-shaped mug, 5 in. high, about 1775.

One of a set of four Champions Bristol figures of the Elements, 10 in. to 11¼ in. high.

CHANTILLY

Rare Chantilly figure of a Chinaman, circa 1735-40, 14cm. high, damaged.

Rare mid 18th century Chantilly double salt and pepper box in three sections, 25cm. wide.

Rare Chantilly figure of a gardener holding a basket of fruit, circa 1740, 16cm. high.

Chantilly two-handled bowl, 11 in. wide.

CHELSEA

Fine Chelsea Hans Sloane botanical plate.

Rare Chelsea box and cover, 4 in. high, circa 1752-56.

Chelsea candlestick group of birds, circa 1762, 7 in. high.

Chelsea white figure of a musician, 8 in. high, about 1755.

CLARICE CLIFF

Clarice Cliff 'Bizarre' vase, 21cm. high, 1930's.

Clarice Cliff biscuit barrel and cake plate.

Clarice Cliff Toby jug.

Attractive Clarice Cliff 'Bizarre' teapot and cream jug, 1930's.

COALBROOKDALE

Coalbrookdale pot pourri vase, cover and stand, 6¾in. high.

Coalbrookdale two-handled cabinet cup, cover and stand, 5½in. tall.

Coalbrookdale kettle on stand with flower encrusting.

One of a pair of Coalbrookdale baluster vases, 10in. high.

COALPORT

A scarce Coalport cup and saucer with 'bleu de roi' ground.

An unusual late 19th century pink ground Coalport tea caddy, 6in. high.

Henrietta, circa 1750, china figure by Coalport, 7in. high.

Coalport flower-encrusted ewer, 10¼in. high, circa 1830.

COMMEMORATIVE

Commemorative mug, 1838, made for Victoria's coronation, 3¾in. high.

Meat paste jar bearing a print of 'The Landing of The British Army at the Crimea'.

A rare commemorative Bragget pot of large size, possibly by Ralph Simpson, circa 1700, 7¼in. high.

Rare commemorative jug, 5½in. high, probably 1832.

COPELAND

Mid 19th century Copeland plaque painted with a view of the Bay of Naples, 30cm. wide.

Copeland Edward VII memorial vase, 1910, 7in. high.

Copeland Parian figure of Sir Walter Scott, circa 1860, 11¾in. high.

Copeland cow creamer, date code for 1884, 14.5cm. high.

COPELAND & GARRETT

Copeland & Garrett molded jug depicting a Gretna Green marriage, circa 1840.

Copeland & Garrett tureen and stand, circa 1860.

Copeland & Garrett figure of Narcissus by John Gibson, 1846, 31cm. high.

One of a pair of Copeland & Garrett Japan pattern New Stone plates, 21.5cm. diam.

COPELAND SPODE

Copeland Spode tureens and dish, circa 1850.

Part of a Copeland Spode seventeen-piece dessert service.

Late 19th century Copeland Spode cabaret.

COPER

Hans Coper spherical stoneware vase, 1960's, 8½in. high.

A stoneware vase, by Hans Coper, the flattened bowl with slightly swelling sides, 16cm. high.

Hans Coper stoneware vase of rectangular oval section, in milky white glaze, 23cm. high.

Hans Coper stoneware vase with spade-shaped body in stone-gray glaze, circa 1968, 49.8cm. high.

DAVENPORT

Part of a Davenport tea and coffee service, circa 1870, sixty-one pieces.

One of a pair of Davenport oviform vases with caryatid handles, circa 1820, 24.5cm. high.

Part of a Davenport pearl-ware botanical part dessert service, circa 1815, sixteen pieces in all.

A Davenport Longport dessert plate, circa 1770.

DECK

A Theodore Deck large circular wall plaque, 59cm. diam.

Theodore Deck dish, 13¼in. diam., circa 1880.

Late 19th century Theodore Deck duck, 12in. high.

Theodore Deck faience dish, circa 1870, 14¼in. diam.

DELFT

A rare 18th century delft Unguent pot, 2¾in. diam.

Rare delft mug, mid 18th century, 4½in. high.

Rare delft Monteith bowl, 13¾in. diam., about 1700-10.

Late 18th century delft dish, 13in. diam.

DELFT, BRISTOL

English delft posset pot, 3½in., circa 1680-90, either Bristol or Brislington.

Bristol delft polychrome blue dash portrait charger, circa 1710, 34cm. diam.

Bristol delft blue and white two-handled jar, 6¼in. high.

Bristol delft flower-brick, circa 1740, 6in. wide.

DELFT, DUTCH

Fine Dutch Delft tea kettle and cover, 25cm. high.

One of a pair of Dutch Delft nine-tiered tulip vases, circa 1690, 5ft.3in. high.

Late 18th century Dutch Delft group of double salts, 30cm. wide.

Dutch Delft bottle, early 18th century, 22.2cm. high.

DELFT, ENGLISH

One of a pair of English delft meat chargers, 20in. long.

Small English delftware cistern and cover, 1644, 14in. high, probably by Christian Wilhelm.

One of a pair of 18th century English delftware wet drug jars.

Delft mug, about 1750, English or Dutch, 7¼in. high.

DELFT, IRISH

Late 18th century, rare, delftware strainer bowl, 8½in. diam.

Rare Irish delft plate, 9¼in., about 1760.

One of a pair of rare Dublin delft vases, late 18th century, 3¾in. high.

Dublin delftware meat dish, Delamain's factory, circa 1760, 43cm. high.

DELFT, LAMBETH

Lambeth delft flower-brick painted in cobalt blue, 15.5cm. wide, circa 1760.

Early Lambeth blue and white apothecary's pill slab, 1687.

Early 18th century Lambeth delft globular jar, 5¼in. diam.

Mid 18th century Lambeth polychrome delft plate, 33.3cm. diam.

DELFT, LIVERPOOL

Very rare late 18th century Liverpool delft leaf dish, 5½in. high.

Large Liverpool delft polychrome baluster vase and domed cover, circa 1760, 49.5cm. high.

Liverpool delft sweetmeat dish, 8¼in., about 1750.

Liverpool delft jug, circa 1760-70, 7¾in. high.

DELFT, LONDON

Late 17th century London delft fuddling cup, 3¼in. high.

17th/18th century London delft barber's bowl, 10in. diam.

Rare London delft figure of a cat.

Late 17th century London delft posset pot and cover, 5¾in. high.

DELLA ROBBIA

Della Robbia vase with three tubular loop handles, galleon D. R. and artist's initials on base, 32cm. high.

Della Robbia pottery vase decorated by Cassandra Ann Walker, 1903, 10in. high.

A fine Della Robbia majolica dish decorated with a border of stags.

Della Robbia vase of pear shape with two loop handles, circa 1898, 14¼in. high.

DE MORGAN

William De Morgan luster saucer dish, Fulham period, 36cm. diam.

De Morgan vase, 1888-97, 9¼in. high, painted by Joe Juster.

De Morgan jardiniere, bell body with twin lug handles, 21.5cm. high.

A De Morgan copper luster goblet, 10.5cm. high.

DERBY

Derby documentary oval plaque with portrait of Shakespeare, 1839, 10.5cm. high, in giltwood frame.

Pair of Derby 'Mansion House' dwarfs, 6¾in. high, about 1820.

Derby 'Tithe Pig' group, by Stevenson & Hancock, circa 1865, 22cm. high.

Derby plate, painted by William Slater Snr., circa 1825, 23cm. diam.

DERBY, BLOOR

One of a pair of Bloor Derby sauce tureens, covers and stands, 8½in. wide.

One of a pair of Bloor Derby ice pails, circa 1830, 12in. high.

Bloor Derby floral encrusted bough pot and cover.

Early 19th century Bloor Derby veilleuse in three parts, 22.5cm. high.

DERBY, ROYAL CROWN

Part of a forty-piece Royal Crown Derby tea service, dated for 1898.

Royal Crown Derby slender two-handled oviform vase and cover, 14½in. high.

Royal Crown Derby plate, dated for 1882, 8¾in. diam.

One of a pair of Royal Crown Derby vases and covers, dated for 1903.

DOCCIA

Doccia rectangular plaque modelled as portrait busts, circa 1745-50, 12.5cm. high.

One of a pair of Doccia blue and white moutardieres, 11.5cm. high, circa 1760.

Rare Doccia bust of the Roman Emperor Augustus, 1750-60, 51cm. high.

Doccia white mythological group of Venus and Adonis with Cupid, circa 1748, 23cm. high.

DOULTON

Early Doulton stoneware candlestick group, 1879, 16cm. high.

Doulton stoneware biscuit barrel, 6¾in. high, dated 1880.

Doulton stoneware teapot, 6¾in. high, dated 1878, with silver lid.

Doulton stoneware oil-lamp base, 11¾in. high, dated 1882.

DOULTON, ROYAL

Royal Doulton jug of a Regency beau.

Unusual Royal Doulton 'Sung' vase, painted by Arthur Charles Eaton, 25cm. high, impressed 6-25.

One of a pair of Royal Doulton vases, by Emma Shute, 21cm. high.

Royal Doulton 'Fox Hounds' presentation jug, 13in. high, dated 1930.

DRESDEN

Part of an early 20th century Dresden coffee service of forty-three pieces.

Late 19th century Dresden gilt metal mounted tankard, 25cm. high.

A large pair of Dresden figures of a gentleman playing bagpipes and his companion with a hurdy-gurdy, 47cm. high.

Dresden 'Naples' sedan chair, sides and door inset with beveled glass windows, circa 1900, 28cm. high.

EARTHENWARE

Large Carrier Belleuse earthenware jardiniere, circa 1900, 38.5cm. high.

Wiener Werkstatte glazed earthenware triple vase, 23cm. high, circa 1910/20.

Cadinen glazed earthenware jug, 1910-20, 19.75cm. high.

Metal mounted D'Argyl Art Deco decorated earthenware vase, 28cm. high, 1920's.

EUROPEAN

Swiss tin glazed chest of drawers, 17.5cm. high.

Saintonage oval dish, 17th century, 31cm. long.

Copenhagen stoneware figure of a child with a cat, modeled by Knud Kyhn.

Large Tournai dish decorated at The Hague, circa 1780, 40cm. diam.

FAENZA

Dated Italian Faenza basket of oval shape, 1613, 23cm. wide.

Early 16th century Faenza drug jar, 22.5cm. high, restored.

Italian Faenza dish, dated 1537, 47cm. diam.

Faenza drug jar, circa 1500, 29.3cm. high, decorated in blue, green and ocher.

FRANKENTHAL

Frankenthal coffee pot, circa 1760, 10¼in. high.

Early Frankenthal arched rectangular tea caddy and cover painted with large birds, circa 1756, 16cm. high.

Frankenthal mythological figure of the Rape of Prosperine, modeled by J.F. Luck, circa 1756, 28cm. high.

A Frankenthal figure of a fruit seller, 14cm. high, 1759-62.

FRENCH

One of a pair of French porcelain cache pots, late 19th century, 16cm. high.

Galle faience seated cat with black glazed body, 33cm. high.

Late 19th century French faience rhinoceros tureen and cover.

20th century French porcelain tisaniere, 9in. high.

FULHAM

Mid 18th century Fulham stoneware mug with foliage encrusted decoration.

One of a pair of C. J. C. Bailey Fulham pottery stoneware vases, 16½in. high, dated 1880.

Late Fulham period De Morgan luster dish painted in ruby and salmon pink, circa 1900, 36.6cm. diam.

Rare Fulham stoneware posset pot, 17th century, 6¾in. high.

FURSTENBERG

Furstenberg shaped oblong gold mounted etui, circa 1760, 11cm. long.

Part of a Furstenberg part coffee service of twelve pieces decorated with flowers, circa 1775.

Late 18th century Furstenberg figure of a fisherman, 12.5cm. high.

GERMAN

German faience Hanau blue and white two-handled octagonal jardiniere.

German porcelain cream jug in the form of a dog, circa 1900.

Late 19th century German porcelain epergne, embossed with flowers, 18in. high, damaged.

South German faience pewter mounted tankard, circa 1744, 20cm. high.

GOLDSCHEIDER

Goldscheider earthenware mask, modeled as a woman, 1920's, 30.5cm. high.

Goldscheider pottery figure of a young girl with flowers, 39.8cm. high.

Large porcelain figure by Friedrich Goldscheider of a young man seated on a chair, 21in. high.

Goldscheider 'bat girl' with winged cape, 1930's, 46.25cm. high.

GOSS

A fine and rare Goss model of a polar bear.

Goss mask head vase, 'Dew Drops', 12.5cm. high.

Early 20th century Goss model of John Knox's House, 4in. high.

Rare late 19th century Goss figure of Lady Betty with flowers and a shawl, 6¾in. high.

HOCHST

Hochst teapot and cover, circa 1765-70, 10.2cm. high.

Hochst figure of a bird-nester by Joh. P. Melchior, 18cm. high, circa 1765-75.

Hochst tea caddy and cover possibly painted by Heinrich Usinger, circa 1770, 14cm. high.

Hochst figure of a young boy modeled by J.P. Melchior, circa 1770, 12cm. high.

ITALIAN

Late 18th century Italian group, 18.5cm. high.

Early Ginori armorial beaker and saucer, circa 1745.

Late 18th century Marcolini part coffee service.

Late 17th century Montelupo dish painted in bright colors, 13in. diam.

JONES

Victorian majolica sardine dish, by George Jones.

Good 'majolica' camel vase, probably George Jones, circa 1870, 9½in. high.

Boxed coffee set of six cups and six saucers, by George Jones, circa 1891.

George Jones 'majolica' jardiniere, 19½in. high, dated 1876.

LEACH

Bernard Leach stoneware vase of bulbous form, circa 1935, 18.5cm. high.

Bernard Leach stoneware 'Pilgrim' dish, 1960's, 12½in. diam.

Bernard Leach stoneware bottle vase, 1960's, 7¾in. high.

St. Ives preserve pot and cover decorated by Bernard Leach, 11.5cm. high.

LEEDS

A figure of a Leeds pearlware stallion, 16¼in. high, circa 1790.

Leeds pearlware group of Venus and Cupid, late 18th century, 7¾in. high.

Late 18th century Leeds creamware cruet stand and bottles, 11in. high.

Leeds creamware ship-decorated plate, circa 1800-1820, 9¾in. diam.

LE NOVE

Le Nove group of two boys and a girl round a tree stump, circa 1780, 18cm. high.

One of three Le Nove teabowls and saucers painted with famille rose flowers, circa 1770.

Pair of Le Nove figures of a lady and a gentleman, circa 1790, 15cm. high.

Le Nove figure of a girl, emblematic of Spring, circa 1775, 13cm. high.

LIMOGES

Limoges enameled pot **and cover, 1920's, 11.5cm., by Sarlandie.**

13th century Limoges head of a crozier, showing the stoning of St. Stephen.

Limoges fish service of twelve plates, a sauceboat and salmon dish, circa 1910.

Limoges porcelain vase, by L. Bernardaud & Cie., 14.5cm. high, circa 1923.

LIVERPOOL

Liverpool blue and white meat dish, 14½in.

Large pottery jug, perhaps Liverpool, 13½in. high, about 1800.

Liverpool blue and white pear-shaped coffee pot, 8½in. high.

Liverpool blue and white shell-shaped pickle dish, 4¼in. wide.

LONGTON HALL

Longton Hall blue and white teabowl and saucer, circa 1755.

One of a pair of Longton Hall figures of seated nuns, chipped, circa 1775.

Longton Hall leaf-shaped bowl, 3in. diam., about 1755.

Rare Longton Hall 'oak leaf' dish, circa 1754-57, 8½in. wide.

LOWESTOFT

Attractive miniature Lowestoft teabowl and saucer in underglaze blue, circa 1760-65.

Lowestoft porcelain figures of musicians, circa 1780-90, 17.8cm. high.

Two very rare Lowestoft blue and white knife and fork handles.

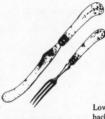

Lowestoft jug with kick-back handle and pink border, 3¼in. high, circa 1785.

LUDWIGSBURG

Ludwigsburg group of a river god, circa 1770, 20cm. wide.

Ludwigsburg arched rectangular tea caddy with Ozier border, circa 1765, 12.5cm. high.

Ludwigsburg porcelain teapot, spherical shape tapering to base, circa 1775, 4¾in. high.

Late 19th century Ludwigsburg group of figures, 25.5cm. high.

LUSTER

Edwardian silver luster teapot and stand.

Good Clement luster charger, circa 1900, 48cm. diam.

Victorian luster ware goblet with fern decoration, 6in. high.

Rare pink luster jug, 13cm. high, circa 1800-1810.

MACINTYRE

Unusual Moorcroft Macintyre jardiniere, circa 1900, 7in. high.

Florian vase made at Macintyres, circa 1893.

One of a pair of Moorcroft Macintyre vases with gilt details and high loop handles, circa 1900, 12.5cm. high.

One of a pair of Moorcroft Macintyre Florianware vases of double gourd shape, signed, 28cm. high.

MAJOLICA

Sicilian majolica bottle, 24cm. high.

Large late 19th century majolica jardiniere with a stand.

One of a pair of majolica ewer jugs, 19in. high.

Interesting early majolica dish, mid 13th century, 19cm. diam.

MARSEILLES

Marseilles faience deep dish, slightly chipped, 31cm. diam., circa 1770.

A Marseilles faience two-handled tureen and cover painted in colors with bouquets of flowers, 36cm wide.

A large early 18th century Marseilles charger decorated with a biblical scene.

A fine Marseilles faience plate, with fish and lobster design.

MARTINWARE

A Martinware jug of gourd shape, 16.5cm. high.

Martin Brothers face jug, 7in. high, incised marks and dated 1903.

Martin Brothers bird, 9¾in. high, incised signature, dated 7-1892.

Martin Brothers stoneware jug, 9¾in. high, incised signature, dated 3-1895.

MASON'S

Mason's inkstand, circa 1830-40.

Impressive Mason's porcelain vase, circa 1810, 25½in. high.

Mid 19th century plate from a Mason's Ironstone part service of ten pieces.

Large hexagonal pot pourri vase, cover and liner, perhaps Mason's, 10½in. high, about 1815-20.

MEISSEN

Early Meissen bowl and cover, 10cm. high, circa 1730.

Meissen group modeled by J. J. Kaendler, 1744, 8½in. high.

Meissen milk jug, in the manner of C. F. Herold.

A large late 19th century Meissen group of Count Bruhl's tailor, 43cm. high.

MENNECY

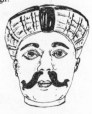

One of a fine pair of ormolu mounted Mennecy figures.

Mid 18th century Mennecy snuff box, 7cm. high, with silver mounts.

Mennecy figure of a Turk carrying a cap and two bags, circa 1750, 16cm. high.

Mid 18th century Mennecy mustard pot and cover, 10cm. high.

METTLACH

Mettlach earthenware vase, tapering at base and neck, circa 1905, 25.25cm. high.

Mettlach plaque decorated after J. Stahl, circa 1900, 46.8cm. diam.

One of a pair of German Mettlach jardinieres, 23in. wide, signed Warth.

Large Mettlach ewer decorated with central frieze, 46cm. high, circa 1900.

CHINA

MINTON

Mid 19th century Minton majolica teapot, 5in. high.

Minton bowl held up by two cherubs, 9in. high.

Rare Minton 'malachite' ewer with loop handle, 35cm. high, dated for 1862.

Minton 'globe pot-pourri' vase, cover and stand, painted with a scene of Hereford, circa 1825-30, 24.5cm. high.

MOORCROFT

Moorcroft vase in 'Moonlit' Blue' Hazeldene pattern, 9¼in. high, 1920-30.

Part of an eleven-piece Moorcroft coffee service in Hazeldene pattern.

Moorcroft twin-handled vase, 11½in. diam., dated 1912.

Moorcroft loving cup of broad cylindrical shape, flaring at rim, signed, 19cm. high.

MOTTOWARE

A Dartmouth pottery jug, inscribed 'No road is long with Good Company'.

An Aller Vale pottery hat-pin stand, decorated with ship design.

A tile from the Watcombe pottery, decorated with leaf and flower swirls.

A Barnstaple pottery jug.

MURRAY

A stoneware flared bowl, by Wm. Staite Murray, 21cm. diam.

Early Wm. Staite Murray stoneware vase, 1923, 8½in. high.

Wm. Staite Murray stoneware bowl, circa 1930, 5½in. diam.

A stoneware oviform vase, by Wm. Staite Murray, 21.5cm. high.

NANTGARW

Nantgarw 'London decorated' sucrier and cover, 4in. high, circa 1817-20.

Fine Nantgarw plate decorated with five carnations, 24cm. diam., circa 1817.

Nantgarw shaped oval center dish from the Mackintosh service, circa 1820, 35.5cm. wide.

Rare Nantgarw pedestal dish, 5¾in. high, 1817-20.

NAPLES

19th century white porcelain Naples figure, 10¾in. high, signed.

One of two Naples armorial wet drug jars, 1690, 22cm. high.

Naples dancing group of a young man and a girl, circa 1780, 19.5cm. high.

Dated Naples bottle, 1701, 25.5cm. high.

NEWHALL

 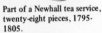

Part of a Newhall tea service, twenty-eight pieces, 1795-1805.

Newhall jug decorated with sprigs of flowers, 4½in. high.

Early 19th century Newhall teapot from a thirty-three piece tea and coffee service.

Newhall jug, circa 1787.

NIDERVILLE

  **NOVE**

A Niderville Parian figure of a shepherd boy with dog, 67cm. high.

One of a rare pair of Niderville covered vases, 15¼in. high, circa 1780.

Large Nove Monteith, circa 1780-90, 49.2cm. wide.

Majolica dish made at Nove da Bassano, circa 1770, 15½in. diam.

NYMPHENBURG

Nymphenburg model of a parrot, circa 1850-62, 18.7cm. high.

Nymphenburg figure of a parrot, circa 1765, 15.5cm. high.

Porcelain ice-bucket from the Nymphenburg factory, 6½in. high.

One of a pair of Nymphenburg cabinet cups and saucers, 9cm. high, circa 1830-40.

PARIAN

Jug showing the famous brass quintet of the Distin father and sons, in Parianware, about 1850, 14in. high.

Robinson & Leadbetter colored Parian figure, 12¼in. high, circa 1890.

Interesting Bailey Murrells & Co. Parian figure of Palmerston, circa 1865, 17in. high

Samuel Alcock & Co. figure of the Duke of Wellington, 11in. high, circa 1852.

PARIS

Paris raspberry ground cache-pot, circa 1870, 18.5cm. high.

Pair of 19th century Paris porcelain figures, 24½in. high.

One of a pair of Feuillet decorated Paris cups and saucers, circa 1840.

One of a pair of late 19th century Paris 'Schneeballen' vases and covers, 38cm. high.

PETIT

One of a pair of Jacob Petit vases, circa 1860.

One of a pair of Jacob Petit urn-shaped porcelain wine coolers, 12in. high.

One of a pair of Jacob Petit scent flasks and stoppers, circa 1840, 27cm. high.

One of a pair of Jacob Petit vases, circa 1840, 21.6cm. high.

PILKINGTON

Pilkington's luster vase trian luster vase, decorated by R. Joyce, 18cm. high.

Small Pilkington Royal Lancastrian ovoid jar and cover, 1926, 12cm. high.

Unusual Pilkington Royal Lancastrian plate, 12¾in. diam., dated for 1906.

Pilkington's luster vase with shouldered barrel body, circa 1907, 8in. high.

PLAUE

Plaue-on-Havel frog band of six pieces, circa 1900.

Plaue centerpiece with pierced detachable bowl on a tree trunk stem, circa 1900, 40.5cm. high.

Pair of late 19th century Plaue fruit stands, 35cm. high.

PLYMOUTH

Pair of Plymouth figures depicting a gardener and his companion, 1768-71.

Rare Plymouth teapot and cover, 6½in. high, about 1768-70.

Important Plymouth figure of 'Winter' in the form of a naked boy with a robe.

Plymouth sauceboat with ribbed scroll handle, circa 1770, 14cm. wide.

POOLE

Poole pottery unglazed jug, 8in. high, 1930.

Poole pottery fish glazed in green with a black base, 17in. high.

Carter, Stabler & Adams Poole pottery vase, circa 1930, 9¾in. high.

Carter, Stabler & Adams Poole pottery vase, circa 1930, 10¾in. high.

CHINA

POTSCHAPPEL

Potschappel porcelain fruit basket on stand, circa 1860.

A pair of Dresden vases, by Carl Thierne of Potschappel, 22½in. high.

Large late 19th century Potschappel vase, cover and stand, applied with nymphs, 82cm. high.

One of a pair of late 19th century Potschappel pot-pourri vases and covers, 15cm. high.

PRATTWARE

A Prattware tea caddy depicting George III, 6¼in. high, 1780-90.

Prattware cockerel standing 10in. tall.

Rare Prattware Toby jug, circa 1780-90, 10in. high.

One of a pair of Prattware fox and swan sauceboats, 6½in. high, about 1780-90.

RIDGWAY

Part of a Ridgway dessert service, circa 1825, nineteen pieces.

Part of a twenty-one piece dessert service, circa 1825-35.

Large Ridgway parian group of Venus and Cupid, 1858, 18¾in. high

One of a pair of Ridgway ice pails, covers and liners, circa 1815-20.

RIE

A porcelain bowl, by Lucie Rie, of wide conical form, 23.5cm. diam.

A stoneware vase by Lucie Rie, covered in cream gray glaze, 30cm. high.

Asymmetrical stoneware vase, by Lucie Rie, 8¼in. high.

Early Lucie Rie earthenware vase of slightly flared form, 1932, damaged, 19.7cm. high.

ROCKINGHAM

Unusually plain Rockingham swan.

Rare early 19th century Rockingham group of a shepherdess and a sheep, 7in. high.

One of a pair of Rockingham plates, 9in. diam.

A Rockingham style part tea and coffee service of forty-five pieces, circa 1830.

ROOKWOOD

Rookwood pottery standard glaze cornucopia vase with swirl rim, Cincinnati, Ohio, 1892, 6in. high.

Rookwood pottery ewer in sage green clay, Ohio, 1900, 8½in. high.

Rookwood sterling overlay standard glaze jardiniere, Ohio, circa 1907, 5½in. high.

Rookwood bisque Spanish water jug, Ohio, circa 1883, 9½in. high.

ROSENBERG

Rosenberg 'eggshell' bowl and cover, decorated by Roelof Sterken, 12cm. high, 1901.

Rosenberg 'eggshell' beaker and saucer, decorated by Sam Schellink, 1904.

Rosenberg 'eggshell' vase with basket handle.

Rosenberg 'eggshell' porcelain cup and saucer by Samuel Schellink, 1903.

ROYAL COPENHAGEN

Copenhagen snuff box and cover modeled as the head of a dog, circa 1793, 6.5cm. wide.

A Royal Copenhagen porcelain oviform vase and cover designed by Ch. Thomasen, 21cm. high.

A Royal Copenhagen group of St. Paul slaying the Lie, circa 1925, 24½in. high.

A Royal Copenhagen porcelain vase of double gourd shape, 21cm. high.

ROYAL DUX

Royal Dux group of a peasant and a bull, circa 1910, 33cm. wide.

Royal Dux Art Deco lady.

Royal Dux camel group, applied pink triangle, circa 1910, 45.5cm. high.

Royal Dux figure group of a family, circa 1880, 25in. high.

RUSKIN

Ruskin 'high-fired' porcelain shallow bowl and stand, 26cm. diam.

Ruskin high-fired vase, with squat body, dated 1933, 8in. high.

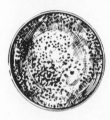

Ruskin high-fired bowl, 4in., dated 1915.

Ruskin Art vase in kingfisher glaze, 10in. high, circa 1913.

RUSSIAN

One of a pair of Russian armorial plates with pierced borders, circa 1870, 25.5cm. diam.

Porcelain group of Hercules and the Nemean lion by Kozlov, Moscow, circa 1830, 18cm. high.

One of a pair of urn-shaped vases by Imperial Porcelain Manufactory, circa 1820, 73cm. high.

Biscuit figure of a man playing an accordion by Gardner, Moscow, circa 1880-90, 18cm. high.

SALTGLAZE

Rare small saltglaze bear mug, 3½in. high, about 1740.

Staffordshire white saltglaze 'house' teapot and cover, circa 1740-50, 6¼in. high.

Staffordshire saltglaze polychrome teapot and cover, with crabstock handle, circa 1755, 20.5cm. wide.

Colored saltglaze cream **jug, 3in. high, about 1760.**

SAMSON

One of a pair of late 19th century ormolu mounted Samson 'Meissen' figures of a Shepherd and Shepherdess, 15.8cm. high.

A Samson pear-shaped coffee pot with domed cover, 21cm. tall.

Samson group of the Levee du Roi of five figures, 38cm. wide.

Pair of Samson parrots on tree-stumps, repaired, 42cm. high.

SCHELLINK

SAVONA

Late 17th century Savona drug jar and cover, 34cm. high.

Early 17th century Savona tazza, 25.5cm. diam.

Rosenberg 'eggshell' vase, decorated by Sam Schellink, 1904, 21.5cm. high.

Rosenberg 'eggshell' vase decorated by Sam Schellink, 1904, 34cm. high.

SEVRES

A Sevres cabinet plate painted by D. Ceniers, late 19th century, 24cm. diam.

An unusual 18th century Sevres bleu du roi ewer, 25.2cm. high.

A Sevres hard paste cup and saucer, circa 1870.

Sevres hexafoil two-handled seau a verre from the Du Barry service, 16.5cm. wide.

SITZENDORF

19th century three branch Sitzendorf candelabrum.

Sitzendorf table centerpiece with pierced basket, 29cm. high.

Late 19th century Sitzendorf clockcase, 38cm. high.

One of a pair of Sitzendorf candelabra, 19½in. high.

SLIPWARE

Staffordshire slipware dish by William Simpson, circa 1700, 34cm. diam.

Slipware baking dish with typical notched rim.

Slipware puzzle jug with pear-shaped body, 14cm. high.

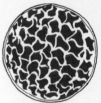

Staffordshire slipware baking dish, freely decorated with a netting pattern.

SPODE

Spode cup and saucer, pattern 967, circa 1810.

Spode pastille burner and cover, circa 1830, 4in. high.

Spode's Imperial covered teapot with gadrooned and leaf moldings, circa 1810.

Spode pink ground oviform vase with loop handles, circa 1820, 18.5cm. high.

STAFFORDSHIRE

Staffordshire group of Alliance, 11in. high, circa 1854.

Staffordshire jug with pictorial decoration.

Staffordshire portrait bust of George Washington, 21cm. high.

Staffordshire figure of Sir Robert Peel, circa 1850, 12¼in. high.

STONEWARE

19th century stoneware quart jug with embossed scenic decoration.

Victorian Gothic castle candleholder of glazed stoneware, 11½in. high.

Tall stoneware flagon with broad strap handle, stamped R. Merkelbach, Grenzhausen, 37.5cm. high.

Stoneware urn, circa 1860, 36in. high.

SUNDERLAND

Mid 19th century Sunderland luster frog mug.

Rare jug of ovoid form, with pink luster neck, probably Sunderland, about 1815.

Rare Sunderland luster pitcher, 1817, 8in. high.

Sunderland luster jug, circa 1840, 7¼in. high.

SWANSEA

Swansea 'bisque' ram, 4¼in. long, 1817-21.

Swansea plate painted with a view of Pembroke Castle.

Swansea inkwell, 4in. diam., 1814-22.

Swansea cabinet cup and saucer, painted by Wm. Pollard, circa 1820.

TERRACOTTA

Italian polychrome terracotta bust of Pope Leo X, early 16th century, 37.5cm. high.

South Italian terracotta modello, 10in. high, circa 1680-1700.

Late 18th century French terracotta group, 15½in. high.

French terracotta figure of Venus, 20in. high, circa 1785.

TOURNAI

Tournai 'Drageoire' or sweetmeat bowl, circa 1760, 15cm. high.

Tournai white group of two boys collecting flowers, circa 1770, 18.5cm. high.

Tournai lobed circular soup plate painted in the manner of Fidelle Duvivier, circa 1765, 24cm. diam.

One of a pair of Tournai pot-pourri vases and covers, mid 18th century, 25.5cm. high.

TURNER

Turner blue and white jasper rectangular plaque, 8 x 5½in.

Large Turner biscuit jug, circa 1800, 8¼in. high.

URBINO

Urbino majolica dish showing the story of Pluto and Prosperine, circa 1530, 12in. diam.

One of a pair of Urbino waisted pharmacy jugs, painted with Bishop's miters, circa 1590, 19cm. high.

VENICE

Venice two-handled beaker vase on spreading foot, circa 1770, 10cm. high.

Early 16th century 'majolica' vase, Venetian.

A rare Venice Vezzi teapot and cover.

One of a pair of Venice puce scale tea bowls and saucers, circa 1770, with shaped borders.

VIENNA

Late 19th century Vienna decorated Eaas and Czjzcr Schlaggenwald plaque, 50.3cm. diam.

One of a pair of late Vienna bleu du roi ground oval two-handled vases, covers and stands, 14in. high.

A Vienna group of an old man and a young girl, 13cm. high, circa 1765.

Early Vienna Du Paquier famille rose globular two-handled pot and cover, 1720-25, 22.5cm. high.

VINCENNES

Vincennes jug with elaborate gilt border, circa 1750-55, 23.5cm. high.

Vincennes white chinoiserie group, circa 1745, 19in. wide.

Vincennes porcelain covered supper dish, circa 1755, 8¼in. wide.

One of a pair of Vincennes porcelain baskets of flowers, 14in. high.

VOLKSTEDT

Late 19th century Eckert & Co. Volkstedt group, 22cm. high.

Well modeled Volkstedt group emblematic of song, circa 1910, 28.3cm. high.

Pair of Volkstedt figures of a Gallant and his Companion, circa 1900, 41cm. high.

Volkstedt centerpiece, late 19th century, 37cm. high.

VYSE, CHARLES

Stoneware foliate bowl, by Charles Vyse, 7¼in. diam.

Charles Vyse figure of 'Barnet Fair', circa 1933, 10¼in. high.

Stoneware model of a leopard, by Charles Vyse, Chelsea, 11in. high.

Charles Vyse earthenware figure of 'The Tulip Woman', 10in. high, circa 1922.

WALFORD, JAMES

James Walford hand modeled pottery group of two figures, 26cm. wide.

James Walford stoneware nude, 1950's, 11in. high.

20th century James Walford stoneware model of an hippopotamus head, 6¾in. wide.

James Walford slab-built stoneware figure of a vulture, contemporary, 19.3cm. high.

WEDGWOOD

Unusual Wedgwood three color jasperware teapot, cover and stand, late 19th century.

One of a pair of Wedgwood candlesticks modeled as dolphins, late 18th century, 10in. high.

Late 19th century Wedgwood black-basalt Portland vase, 11in. high.

Wedgwood 'Rosso Antico' D-shaped bulb pot and cover, 7¼in. wide.

WEMYSS

Small Wemyss conserve pot and cover, painted with cherries, 7.5cm. high, with matching stand.

Wemyssware molded jug, circa 1910, 8in. high.

Wemyss cone shaped base with four ring handles, 13cm. high.

Part of a Robert Heron & Son Wemyssware toilet set, 20th century.

WESTERWALD

Rare 18th century Westerwald tankard, inscribed 'London', 18.5cm. high.

Early 18th century Westerwald salt cellar with salt-glaze, 17cm. high.

Rare 18th century Westerwald part writing set modeled as lions, 17.7cm. high.

Westerwald jug with flattened globular body, 1641, with replacement metal handle, 31.5cm. high.

WHIELDON

Whieldon green glazed rectangular tea caddy, circa 1760, 11.5cm. high.

Whieldon cow creamer and cover, circa 1760, 5¼in. high.

Whieldon oviform teapot and cover with crabstock spout and handle, circa 1755, 19cm. wide.

Whieldon type Toby jug circa 1750, 6¼in. high.

WOLFSOHN

Late 19th century Helena Wolfsohn liqueur set, stand 28cm. wide.

One of a pair of Helena Wolfsohn Dresden covered vases.

Late 19th century set of Helena Wolfsohn monkey bandsmen.

Late 19th century pair of Helena Wolfsohn bottles and covers, 33cm. high.

WOOD, ENOCH

Massive Enoch Wood pearlware jug, late 18th century, 17in. high.

Enoch Wood figure of a roaring lion, circa 1790, 12¼in. wide.

Rare Enoch Wood figure of John Liston, 6¼in. high, about 1820.

One of a set of six Enoch Wood creamware plates, 10in. diam., about 1790.

WOOD, RALPH

Rare and attractive Ralph Wood elephant spill vase, circa 1770-80, 8in. high.

An inscribed and dated Ralph Wood jug of large size, modeled by Jean Voyez, 9½in. high, 1788.

Late 18th century model of a squirrel in the style of Ralph Wood.

Late 18th century Ralph Wood Toby jug, 24.5cm. high.

WORCESTER

Worcester straight-sided mug with transfer-printed border, circa 1770.

Worcester 'Beckoning Chinaman' teapot and cover, 6in. high, about 1755-58.

A Worcester fluted coffee cup and saucer, 1765-70.

Worcester coffee pot and cover, 23.5cm. high.

WORCESTER, CHAMBERLAIN

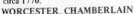

Chamberlain Worcester card tray with painted center.

Chamberlain Worcester figure of one of the Rainer Brothers, 6in. high, about 1830.

Fine Chamberlain's Worcester ice pail, cover and liner, on square marble base, 35cm. wide.

Chamberlain Worcester vase and cover of baluster shape, 46cm. high.

WORCESTER, DR. WALL

A Dr. Wall period hot water jug complete with cover.

One of a pair of Dr. Wall First period Worcester porcelain plates, 8¾in. diam.

Worcester Dr. Wall period tea caddy and cover decorated with flowers and insects, 4¼in. tall.

Dr. Wall Worcester teapot, 6in. high, with scale blue base.

WORCESTER, FLIGHT, BARR & BARR

One of a pair of Flight, Barr & Barr claret ground plates, circa 1820, 22.5cm. diam.

One of a pair of Worcester Flight, Barr & Barr period lidded vases, 11in. high.

Inkstand by Flight, Barr and Barr, 5½in., full script mark in sepia, 1815-20.

Worcester teapot marked Flight, Barr & Barr, 1807-13.

WORCESTER, GRAINGER

Model of a giraffe by Grainger, Lee & Co., 4½in. high, on oval gilt base.

One of a garniture of three Grainger Worcester pot pourri vases, circa 1815, 13½in. and 10¾in. high.

Grainger, Lee & Co. part dinner service, twenty-four pieces, 1812-20.

Grainger's Worcester vase and cover, dated for 1901, 9¼in. high.

WORCESTER, HANCOCK

Worcester punch bowl with scene of a foxhunt by Robert Hancock, 11in. diameter, 1760-65.

Fine Worcester jug printed by Hancock, 7¼in. high, circa 1760.

Fine English circular basket by Robert Hancock, 7¾in. diam., about 1765.

Rare English porcelain mug by Robert Hancock, 4½in. high, about 1760-65.

WORCESTER, ROYAL

Royal Worcester vase, circa 1880, with molded woven body, 8in. high.

Royal Worcester teapot and cover, 6in. high, dated for 1882.

Royal Worcester ewer with squat domed body, 1887, 4½in. high.

Royal Worcester basket in the form of a bird's nest, circa 1890, 6in. high.

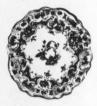

Royal Worcester plate, dated for 1912, 9in. diam.

One of a pair of Royal Worcester vases, 9¾in. high, dated for 1913,

Pair of Royal Worcester sugar sifters, 6¾in. high, circa 1898.

Royal Worcester vase and cover, 1899.

YORKSHIRE

Late 18th century Yorkshire 'squat' Toby jug, with caryatid handle, 7¼in. high.

A rare Yorkshire equestrian figure, 8¾in. high, circa 1780.

Yorkshire pottery group, 9in. high, circa 1780-90.

Yorkshire figure of a cockerel splashed in brown, ocher, yellow and blue, circa 1780, 16.5cm. high.

ZURICH

Zurich porcelain figure representing Painting, 6½in. high.

Mid 18th century Zurich plate, 23cm. diam.

Pair of 18th century Zurich porcelain figures representing Autumn, 8½in. high.

Zurich jug with scroll molded spout, circa 1765, 12.5cm. high.

ARITA

Fine 18th century Arita blue and white hexagonal lobed bowl with floral design, Fuku mark, 21.2cm. diam.

17th century Japanese Arita blue and white lidded porcelain jar, 13in. high.

Late 17th century Arita dog decorated in black, iron red and turquoise green, 23cm. long.

One of a pair of Imari Arita porcelain bottles, circa 1700.

BLUE & WHITE

A late 18th century Chinese blue and white porcelain tankard, 5¼in.

Mid 17th century Chinese blue and white porcelain vase, 8¼in. high.

Mid 19th century Japanese blue and white porcelain dish, 14½in. diam.

Early 19th century blue and white bidet of pear-shape, 61.5cm. long.

CANTON

Late 19th century Canton teapot with floral decoration.

One of a pair of Canton famille rose vases, mid 19th century, 35cm. high.

Canton dish, typically painted and gilt, 35cm. diam., circa 1870.

A large early 19th century Canton enamel jardiniere, decorated with scenic views.

CHENGHUA

Chinese porcelain jar of the Chenghua period, decorated in underglaze blue, 10.3cm

Chenghua stem cup decorated in iron-red and underglaze blue, with various fabulous animals, 4in. high.

Blue and white porcelain saucer dish from the reign of Chenghua, 8in. diam.

Doucai wine cup decorated in blue, red, yellow and pale green, with six character mark of Chenghua.

CHINESE

Chinese white porcelain ewer of the Liao dynasty with a simulated cane work handle.

Chinese Jizhou teabowl with brown glaze, 11.5cm. diam.

One of a pair of apple-green Chinese porcelain vases, 13¾in. high.

20th century Chinese porcelain fish tank decorated with birds and flowers.

DAOGUANG

Small, Daoguang period, famille rose ruby ground bowl with floral decoration and scenic views in panels.

Chinese porcelain orchid vase of the Daoguang period.

Daoguang blue and white circular sweetmeat dish and cover, 13½in. diam.

Baluster shaped porcelain vase decorated with famille rose enamels, Daoguang period, 7¼in.

EDO

Early Edo period seto chaire with ivory cover, 5.5cm. high

Mid Edo period Tamba 'moxa' chaire with ivory lid, 11cm. high.

EXPORTWARE

18th century Chinese export charger, 12½in. diam.

Oriental export porcelain chocolate pot, late 18th century, 10in. high.

EXPORTWARE

18th century Chinese export porcelain documentary punchbowl.

Pair of 19th century export figures of an Emperor and Empress.

Famille rose porcelain export jug and cover, Qianlong, 24cm. high.

18th century Chinese export porcelain Masonic tankard.

FAMILLE NOIRE

Mid 19th century famille noire vase with waisted neck, 53.5cm. high.

One of a pair of large Chinese famille noire pear-shaped vases painted with dignitaries and immortals, 21¾in. high.

18th century famille noire porcelain vase of baluster form, 52cm. high.

Famille noire tapering square vase, 20¾in. high.

FAMILLE ROSE

One of a pair of mid 19th century Chinese famille rose jars and covers.

Famille rose porcelain plate, 8¾in. diam., decorated with blossom, insects and plants, late 18th century.

Mid 19th century well painted famille rose screen with carved hardwood stand, 55cm. high.

18th century famille rose fish tank, 23in. diam.

FAMILLE VERTE

One of a pair of famille verte brushwashers and water droppers.

Pair of famille verte Immortals, 18½in. high.

Late 19th century famille verte vase and cover with baluster body, 43cm. high.

A famille verte tea caddy decorated with vases and flowers.

FUKAGAWA

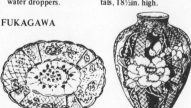

One of a pair of lobed Fukagawa bowls, circa 1900, 10¼in. long.

One of a pair of Fukagawa vases with colored enamels, circa 1900, 13in. high.

One of a pair of Fukagawa Imari bottle vases with red grounds, circa 1900, 30cm. high.

One of a pair of late 19th century Fukagawa vases and covers, 16in. high.

GUAN

Guan compressed jar with crackleware glaze, 4¼in. high.

18th century Guan type vase, 6in. high.

HAMADA

A stoneware circular dish, by Shoji Hamada, 32cm. diam.

A stoneware flared vase, by Shoji Hamada, 19.5cm. high.

HAN

Han dynasty unglazed pottery triceratops, 10½in. long.

Rare green glazed model of a stove of the Han dynasty.

Unglazed pottery head from the Han dynasty, 4in. high.

Rare Han dynasty green glazed pottery cauldron and cover, 20.2cm. wide.

HICHOZAN

One of a pair of Hichozan Shinpo bottle vases, late 19th century, 10in. high.

Late 19th century Hichozan Shinpo vase, 49.5cm. high, with pierced neck.

HIRADO

19th century Hirado porcelain inro of four cases, unmarked.

Hirado blue and white ewer and cover modeled as a seated boy holding a dog.

HODODA

Hododa Kinkozan earthenware vase in the form of a phoenix, 1890, 14.5cm. high.

Hododa earthenware bowl painted and gilt, circa 1900, 31cm. diam.

HOZAN

One of a pair of Hozan earthenware vases, circa 1900, 6¼in. high.

Late 19th century Hozan Satsuma dish with fluted rim, 10in. diam.

IMARI

Late 17th century green ground Imari wine ewer, 15.5cm. high.

Imari porcelain goldfish bowl with floral decoration, 20in. diam.

Japanese Imari vase from the late 19th century, 62cm. high.

Fine Japanese Imari charger, 23½in. diam.

JAPANESE

Late 19th century Japanese charger painted in colored enamels, 22¼in. diam.

Japanese plique a jour vase with gold wire framed enamel decoration.

19th century Japanese tureen and cover in the form of a roosting crane, 26.5cm. wide.

Japanese whisky set with five bowls.

One of a pair of Japanese earthenware flasks, 1880's, 28cm. high.

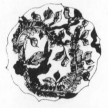

A Japanese dish with hexagonal lotus paneled edge, decorated with a pattern of leaves, 14½in. diam.

One of a pair of Japanese earthenware vases gilt with panels, circa 1900, 30.5cm. high.

Japanese earthenware vase and cover in the form of a rope-tied bag, 22cm. high, circa 1880.

KAKIEMON

Late 17th century Kakiemon wine-pot and cover of ovoid form.

Late 17th century Kakiemon ewer, painted in red, blue and green enamels.

Kakiemon decagonal dish of late 17th century date.

A fine teabowl and saucer painted in the Kakiemon palette, circa 1770.

KANGXI

Kangxi rare underglaze blue and red jardiniere, 8¾in. diam.

One of a pair of Kangxi period famille verte Buddhistic lion joss stick holders, 20.5cm. high.

Kangxi famille verte porcelain plate, 23cm. diam.

Kangxi blue and white stem cup, 5½in. high.

KINKOZAN

Japanese Kinkozan bowl with wavy rim, circa 1870.

Kinkozan earthenware kettle and cover painted and gilt on a blue ground, circa 1900, 13cm. high.

Kinkozan earthenware vase, 17in. high, circa 1870.

A late 19th century Kinkozan plate well painted by Seizan, 20.6cm. high.

KOREAN

Korean inlaid celadon bowl from the Koryo dynasty, 18cm. diam.

Korean Yi dynasty blue and white globular jar, cracked, 8½in. diam.

12th century Korean celadon wine ewer, 7in. high.

Korean Yi dynasty blue and white globular vase painted with peony sprays.

KUTANI

A Kutani vase and cover, a young sake tester modeled on one side, 27cm. high, late 18th century.

Japanese Kutani plate decorated with birds and foliage, 14in. diam.

Late 19th century Kutani drummer boy, 9½in. high.

A Kutani washing set comprising a bowl, jug and two boxes, circa 1900.

MING

16th century Ming jar in blue and white porcelain, 15in. diam.

Chinese wine ewer made in the 14th century and painted in copper red, 12¾in. high.

Early Ming blue and white porcelain flask, 10in. high.

Unusual Ming dynasty celadon group, 9in. high.

MISCELLANEOUS

Mid 16th century Isnik pottery stemmed dish, 12in. diam.

Mid 19th century Tomonobu earthenware koro and cover, 20cm. high.

Late 19th century Kyoto earthenware bowl in the form of a shell, 42.5cm. wide.

Mid 19th century Unzan koro and cover in earthenware, with hexagonal body, 13cm. high.

16th century Annamese saucer dish, painted with underglaze blue.

NANKIN

Ban Chiang gray pottery jar with globular body and flared neck, 2nd/1st millenium B.C., 12in. high.

A Nisshuto Shokai koro and cover, painted with panels of courtesans in a garden, 6.8cm. high, circa 1900.

Rare Namban figure of a bishop carrying a crozier and rosary, 12in. tall.

One of a pair of Nankin style blue and white porcelain vases, 10¾in. high.

Nankin tureen, decorated in polychrome with Oriental garden scenes and with a domed cover.

One of a pair of round blue and white Nankin vases, 24in. high.

Blue and white Nankin tankard with delicate geometric border around rim, the body decorated with a landscape scene, circa 1790, 4½in. high.

QIANLONG

Qianlong period blue and white pilgrim vase, 51cm. high.

Export tureen modeled **as a seated goose**, **Qianlong**, 15¾in. high x 12¾in. wide.

Qianlong blue and white charger decorated with a hunting scene, 17in. diam.

Qianlong incense burner and cover surmounted with a Dog of Fo.

QING

Large late 19th century enameled dish, 59.2cm. diam.

Chinese porcelain cockerel, circa 1800.

A 19th century Chinese jardiniere, 16in. high and 18in. diam.

Celadon vase with central floral panel, circa 1870.

RYOZAN

Late 19th century Unzan Ryozan vase, 12in. high.

A Ryozan earthenware dish enameled and gilt with child acrobats, 15.5cm. high, circa 1900.

A Ryozan Satsuma vase painted with travelers in a bleak snowy landscape, 24cm. high, late 19th century.

One of a pair of Japanese earthenware plates, 23.8cm. diam., circa 1870.

SATSUMA

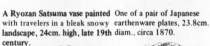

19th century Satsuma decorated teapot, 7½in. high.

Late 19th century Japanese Satsuma vase of baluster form, 12in. high.

Outstanding Japanese Satsuma bowl with a gilt encrusted pictorial scene of the arrival of Chinese envoys, dated 1804.

19th century Satsuma porcelain figure of a boy playing a drum, 38cm. high.

SONG

Song dynasty jar decorated with three stylised leaf sprays, 5¼in. high.

Chinese Cizhou vase of the Song dynasty painted in dark brown and with a leaf green glaze, 26cm. high.

SUI

Sui/early Tang dynasty Changsha glazed stoneware vase and cover with cup-shaped mouth, 13.1cm. high.

Sui dynasty straw glazed equestrian tomb figure, 13in. high.

TANG

A Tang dynasty figure of a horse, 28in. wide.

Tang dynasty rare unglazed figure of a camel groom, 16in. high.

Pair of large unglazed buff pottery figures, Tang dynasty, 32in. high.

Tang dynasty dark green globular storage jar, 7¼in. high.

WANLI

Wanli blue and white saucer dish, 15in. diam.

Wanli blue and white pear-shaped bottle, 27cm. high.

Kraak porcelain dish, Wanli period, circa 1600, 11in. diam.

Chinese Wanli plate decorated with dragons and flowers, 8in. diam.

WEI

Wei dynasty unglazed pottery hound, 6½in. wide.

Early Wei dynasty pottery figures of four tomb attendants, 8in. high.

WUCAI

Fine mid 16th century Ming Wucai jar, 7½in. high.

One of a pair of Ming dynasty Wucai saucer dishes, painted with 'The Three Friends of Winter', 5¾in. diam.

WUCAI

Wucai transitional period jar, circa 1650, 10½in. high.

Very rare Turkish market Wucai bottle in Iznik palette, Kangxi, 23.1cm.

Wucai dragon and phoenix saucer dish with foot rim, 32.1cm. diam., decorated in famille verte.

Fine Wucai baluster vase and cover, circa 1650-70, 14in. high.

XUANDE

A rare blue and white porcelain stem cup and stand of the Xuande period, 4in. high.

One of a pair of Ming stem cups, made in the reign of the Emperor Xuande.

YIXING

Rare Chinese export Yixing figure, 19th century.

18th century Yixing teapot and cover.

YONGZHENG

One of a pair of Yongzheng famille rose fish bowls.

One of a pair of Yongzheng famille rose dishes, 12½in. diam.

Yongzheng or early Qianlong famille rose square vase on short feet, 5in. high.

Yongzheng famille rose porcelain plate decorated with blossom, fish and flowers, 8¾in. diam.

YUAN

Yuan dynasty celadon incense burner, 3¾in. wide.

Early 14th century pale blue wine ewer from the Yuan dynasty, 13¼in. tall.

Rare 14th century Yuan dynasty stem cup stand, 7½in. diam.

Chinese porcelain vase of the Yuan dynasty with pale blue glaze, 28.6cm. high.

BRACKET CLOCKS

19th century bracket clock, 14in. high, in mahogany and brass case.

Quarter repeating oak bracket clock, circa 1900, 16in. high.

Late 18th century mahogany quarter repeating bracket clock by William Dutton, 14in. high.

Eight-day English fusee bracket clock in ebony case by A. Quiguer, London, circa 1687.

Walnut striking bracket clock by Robt. Sadler, London, 14½in. high.

Japanned quarter repeating bracket timepiece, 13½in. high.

A Japanese striking bracket clock, 170mm. high.

Late 18th century musical bracket clock by Robert Ward, London, 61cm. high.

Mid 17th century bracket clock in an ebony veneered case by Pieter Visbagh, 10in. high.

Bracket clock by Thos. Tompion, London, circa 1700, 40cm. high.

George III mahogany bracket clock by Richard Webster, London, 18½in. high.

George III mahogany bracket clock by William Cozens of London, 1ft. 3½in. tall.

George III mahogany bracket clock by John Robert & Silva, London, 2ft.2in. high.

Dutch ebony gilt mounted bracket clock, 17in. high.

Walnut bracket clock by Daniel Quare, London, 14in. high.

Regency mahogany striking bracket clock by Panchaud & Cumming, London, 16in. high.

CARRIAGE CLOCKS

Porcelain mounted carriage clock, 6½in. high.

19th century carriage clock in the Japanese manner.

Late 19th century carriage clock by Nicole Nielson & Co., in silver case, 11.5cm. high.

Clock attributed to Mucha, circa 1900, 9in. high.

French brass striking carriage clock by Maurice & Co., 6½in. high.

Gilt spelter carriage clock, circa 1890, 6½in. high.

Gilt metal oval brass striking carriage clock by Drocourt, 5½in. high.

Grande sonnerie striking carriage clock by Drocourt, Paris.

French brass cased grande sonnerie carriage clock, 7in. high.

Early French gilt metal pendule de voyage, dial signed Dubois, Paris, circa 1780, 7½in. high.

French miniature carriage clock, 3¼in. high, with silvered dial.

English gilt metal carriage timepiece by Viner & Co., London, 4½in. high.

French gilt metal carriage clock, 8½in. high.

19th century petite sonnerie carriage clock by Joseph Berrolla, Paris.

Enamel mounted carriage clock in leather case, 6½in. high.

Elaborate gilt metal striking carriage clock, 8¼in. high.

CLOCK SETS

Gilt spelter clock garniture, circa 1880, clock 14in. high.

Victorian china clock set with transfer decoration.

Gilt bronze clock garniture, clock in the form of an owl, circa 1890.

Gilt bronze and Dresden porcelain clock garniture, circa 1880, clock 14in. high.

Gilt bronze and Sevres clock garniture, circa 1880.

19th century French style clock garniture.

Late 19th century painted spelter and onyx clock garniture.

Ormolu and marble clock garniture, circa 1900, dial signed Camerden and Foster, New York, Made in France.

GRANDFATHER CLOCKS

Small George III mahogany regulator, 6ft.11in. high.

Regency longcase clock with brass dial by N. Barwise, London.

A painted mahogany musical calendar longcase clock, 8ft. 10in. high.

Scottish longcase clock by David Greig, Perth, with shaped case.

French Provincial longcase clock with elaborate brass pendulum.

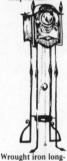

Stylish modernistic clock, 1930's, 112cm. high.

Early 19th century mahogany longcase clock, 94in. high.

Wickerwork longcase clock.

Wrought iron longcase clock, circa 1920, 65½in. high.

Mahogany longcase clock, circa 1830, 93in. high.

Small longcase clock in a walnut marquetry case by J. Wise, circa 1680, 6ft.8in. high.

Mahogany longcase clock by Jn. and Wm. Mitchell, Glasgow, mid 19th century, 83in. high.

Early 19th century longcase clock signed Robin aux Galeries du Louvre, 6ft.10in. high.

Large marquetry chiming clock, circa 1900, 105½in. high.

Late 19th century mahogany longcase clock.

LANTERN CLOCKS

19th century country-made lantern clock, 14in. high.

Provincial lantern clock by E. Bilbie, circa 1675, 10in. high.

Wing alarm lantern clock, 1ft.3in. high.

Small brass lantern time-piece with alarm, circa 1700, 170mm. high.

Lantern clock, circa 1690, by Joseph Windmills, London, 16in. high.

Louis XV Provincial wall timepiece, 14½in. high.

Small lantern clock signed Sam Wichell, Piccadilly, 9in. high.

Balance wheel lantern clock by Baker, complete with doors.

Miniature traveling verge lantern clock by Charles Groode, London.

Alarm lantern clock by Wm. Kipling, London, 1ft.3in. high.

17th century brass lantern clock with one hand.

Small lantern clock, signed Robert Dingley, London, 9in. high.

English brass quarter striking lantern clock, 12¾in. high.

Lantern clock by John Knibb, Oxford, circa 1690, 17½in. high.

Late 17th century brass lantern clock.

18th century Japanese lantern clock, 280mm. high.

MANTEL CLOCKS

Lalique frosted glass clock, 16cm. high, circa 1920.

Early 18th century gilt metal astronomical traveling clock by Wm. Winrowe, 10in. high.

German gilt metal striking table clock, 12.5cm. square.

Gilt metal and marble mantel clock, circa 1880, 13in. high.

19th century Dutch Delft clock with brass works, 18½in. high.

Art Deco bronze and marble clock, 26cm. wide, 1920's.

Mid Victorian mantelpiece clock in brass and bronze mounted case.

Louis XVI white marble and ormolu timepiece, enamel dial signed Schmit a Paris, 1ft.3in. high.

Late 18th century Flemish painted mantel clock, 2ft. 4in. high.

Mid 19th century bronze and marble mantel clock, 21½in. high.

Black Forest organ clock, in Gothic styled oak case, 34½in. high.

20th century walnut cased mantel clock.

Clock case in green marble surmounted by a bronze figure, circa 1900, 39cm. high.

Viennese enameled copper clock, 39cm. high, circa 1910.

Late 19th century clock, with ormolu mounts, 16in. high.

Late 19th century parcel gilt bronze lyre timepiece, with sunburst finial, 15½in. high.

MANTEL CLOCKS

Louis XVI ormolu and white marble mantel clock, 1ft.2in. high.

Mahogany cased clock with tulipwood banding, 25in. high.

Victorian barometer, clock and thermometer in oak case, 13in. high.

Preiss clock with marble base, 1930's, 37cm. high.

Late 19th century ormolu and bronze mantel clock with urn surmount.

Gilt bronze and porcelain mounted mantel clock, circa 1870, 16in. high.

French 19th century mantel clock.

Regency period mahogany cased mantel clock, 13in. high.

Viennese giltwood David and Goliath grande sonnerie mantel clock, 19in. high.

19th century white marble calendar mantel clock, 1ft. 4in. high.

Gilt and patinated bronze mantel clock, circa 1860, 18in. high, surmounted by a group of a Turk and his Horse.

Ithaca parlor model calendar clock in walnut case, with double dial.

French gilt and patinated bronze mantel clock, circa 1850-75, 1ft.10in. high.

Small Liberty & Co. pewter and enamel clock, 19.75cm. high, after 1903.

Ormolu Strutt timepiece with eight-day movement, signed 'Made by Thos. Cole', 5½in. high.

French Empire mantel clock in mahogany case, 50cm. high.

SKELETON CLOCKS

Brass cathedral skeleton clock signed C.Fiedemann, Liverpool.

Brass long duration timepiece skeleton clock, 12¾in. high.

Rare epicyclic skeleton clock, 10in. high, with a glass dome.

Brass skeleton clock, 13in. high.

Early skeleton clock by Hubert Sarton, 1ft. 5½in. high.

Unusual early 19th century skeleton clock of 'rafter' construction.

Large English striking skeleton clock, 22in. high.

Mid 19th century silvered brass skeleton timepiece, 12½in. high.

Rare chiming calendar skeleton clock, 1ft.7in. high.

Skeleton clock by Smith & Sons, Clerkenwell, 1ft. 4½in. high.

Good quality original Victorian skeleton timepiece, circa 1860.

English brass chiming skeleton clock, 20in. high.

Brass skeleton clock with enamel dial, circa 1890, 15¼in. high.

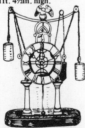

Unusual timepiece skeleton clock, 20in. high, with glass dome.

Unusual long duration Dutch skeleton clock, 2ft. 5in. high.

Astronomical skeleton clock, by James Gorham, 19th century.

WALL CLOCKS

Inlaid American eight day clock, circa 1890, 2ft. 4in. high.

Stained oak wall clock, Austrian, circa 1880, 38in. high.

Elaborate Victorian mahogany framed wall clock with brass pendulum.

Unusual mahogany wall timepiece by James McCabe, London, 8½in. high.

18th century French wall clock, 10½in. high.

Bristol example of an Act of Parliament clock by Wm. Preist.

Early striking clock by James Cowpe, London, circa 1665, 17in. high.

A 17th century Italian night clock in ebony case, 36½ x 22in.

Vienna regulator in dark walnut, 60in. high, circa 1900.

French giltwood cartel clock, signed J. Marti et Cie, 39in. high.

Early 20th century oak cased wall clock.

German Zappler clock, with brass face, 11½in. high.

Dutch Friesland clock with painted dial, 27in. high.

Japanese weight driven wall timepiece, 16in. high.

Victorian papier mache wall clock by E. Fixary.

Mahogany wall regulator dial signed Dent, London, 4ft.4in. high.

WATCHES

Mid 18th century silver pair cased verge watch by Markwick of London, 73mm. diam.

Silver gilt and enamel duplex watch, 56mm. diam.

Silver quarter repeating alarm verge watch, signed Paul Beauvais, London, 55mm. diam.

Gold quarter repeating cylinder watch, by Ellicott of London, 1766, 49mm. diam.

Silver pair cased false pendulum verge watch by Marke Hawkins, 53mm. diam.

17th century verge watch by Joseph Chamberlain, Norwich, 52mm. diam.

Gold and enamel verge watch signed Breguet a Paris, 46mm. diam., circa 1790.

Swiss silver keyless mystery watch signed A. S. & P. Mysterieuse, Brevete S. G. D. G., 53mm. diam.

Swiss gold quarter repeating Jacquemart verge watch, 56mm. diam.

Oval silver watch for the Turkish Market, with Turkish numerals and subsidiary lunar dial, 63mm. long.

Silver pair cased verge watch, signed Thos. Gorsuch, Salop, 56mm. diam.

Silver pair cased verge watch by Markwick, London, circa 1710.

19th century gold quarter repeating independent center seconds lever watch by Lepine, Paris, 47mm. diam.

Large silver pair cased verge watch, signed Wm. Smith, 81mm. diam.

Cartier gold breast pocket clip watch, 1930's, 5.3cm.

Pedometer watch signed by Spencer & Perkins, London, 52mm. diam., circa 1780.

Late 19th century Japanese cloisonne opaque and transparent enamel on copper jar, 3½in. high.

Cloisonne enamel quail, 5in. high, Qianlong period.

Two-handled cloisonne bowl, early 15th century, 8in. wide.

One of a pair of Ch'ien Lung cloisonne enamel boxes and covers, 7in. wide.

Fine 19th century cloisonne two-handled vase, 22in. high.

Early 19th century cloisonne enamel incense burner.

A good late 18th century cloisonne enamel teapot.

19th century Japanese cloisonne enamel vase, 7in. high.

One of a pair of cloisonné and gilt-bronze horses and riders, 12½in. high, 19th century.

One of a pair of cloisonne enamel pricket candlesticks, 19in. high.

19th century Japanese cloisonne dish, 14in., diam.

One of a pair of 19th century ormolu mounted cloisonne enamel vases.

One of a pair of large cloisonne altar candle holders, circa 1900.

Slightly cracked cloisonne vase, with full body enamelled with cranes, circa 1900, 13cm. high.

One of a pair of Japanese cloisonne enamel vases, 36in. high, circa 1900.

One of a pair of cloisonne enamel figures of cocks, 6¾in. high.

One of a pair of Christopher Dresser brass candlesticks, 1880's.

Early 18th century copper wine flagon.

Set of three Victorian brass fire implements.

A large solid copper 19th century wash boiler, 20in. diam.

Brass and lacquer vase by Jean Dunand, circa 1925.

Victorian brass watering can.

Early 19th century brass trivet with wooden handle.

One of a pair of Liberty & Co. brass candlesticks, 13.5cm. high, circa 1900.

Copper jar with a silver cover, surmounted by a lapis lazuli finial.

Unusual copper and wrought iron illuminated heater, 30in. high, circa 1900.

One of a pair of early 17th century brass candlesticks, 12in. high.

W. Benson copper and brass kettle and burner, 11½in. high, 1890's.

Late 16th century Venetian brass charger, 19½in. diam.

19th century brass fireguard.

Late 19th century oak framed brass gong.

A gallon copper measure.

19th century brass chamberstick with drip pan.

Pair of Victorian iron and brass dogs.

Newlyn copper rose bowl, 10¾in. diam., circa 1910.

Late 18th century pierced brass footman with shaped front legs.

Early 17th century North German brass candlestick, 8¼in. high.

French fireman's brass helmet.

20th century pressed brass magazine stand.

Horse brass on leather.

Brass electric kettle designed by Peter Behrens, circa 1920. 22.75cm. high.

Limoges enameled copper dish with transparent red border, circa 1870, 6¾in. long.

Copper and brass jardiniere on stand, Austrian, circa 1910, 53in. high.

Late 19th century brass fire grate, 38in. wide.

Victorian brass trivet with screw on legs.

Late 19th century brass coal scuttle.

Art Deco brass sparkguard carved with a peacock.

19th century Japanese patinated brass teapot of bulbous form with wrapped handle grip, 6in. diam.

German pocket corkscrew in the form of a can-can dancers legs.

Victorian brass and ivory corkscrew.

Unusual brass Victorian corkscrew.

Victorian corkscrew with horn handle and brush, about 1860.

Victorian brass and ivory corkscrew.

Steel rack and pinion hand corking device, 6¼in. high.

Unusual Victorian brass corkscrew.

Single lever corkscrew by Charles Hull, 1864.

One of a pair of Victorian corkscrews.

Victorian steel corkscrew.

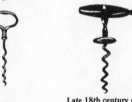

Late 18th century example of the first patented corkscrew.

Late 19th century plated pocket corkscrew.

Unusual Dutch silver corkscrew, 4½in. high.

19th century Plum's patent ratchet corkscrew with ivory handle, brass barrel and steel screw.

Dutch silver corkscrew by Hendrik Smook, Amsterdam 1753.

Mid 19th century rare bronze corkscrew, possibly French.

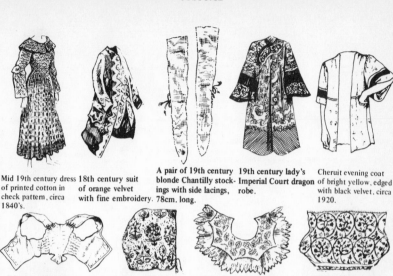

Mid 19th century dress of printed cotton in check pattern, circa 1840's.

18th century suit of orange velvet with fine embroidery.

A pair of 19th century blonde Chantilly stockings with side lacings, 78cm. long.

19th century lady's Imperial Court dragon robe.

Cheruit evening coat of bright yellow, edged with black velvet, circa 1920.

Pair of late 18th century stays of white linen with silk binding, circa 1790.

Carolean linen cap.

Large chain point collar with scallop edge, circa 1840.

Embroidered linen coif, circa 1580-1610.

French beaded dress with slate blue muslin ground, 1920's, skirt with vandyked hem.

Chanel sequinned long evening dress, labeled, circa 1930, zip and bodice added.

Printed silk two-piece bodice and skirt, with purple violet sprigs, circa 1895.

Unusual polychrome and gold thread long satin evening dress with cross-over bodice, 1920's.

Gold lace long evening dress and jacket with roses down the side, 1930's.

Early 17th century kid glove.

Pair of Queen Victoria's bloomers.

19th century Brussels triangular shawl of bobbin and needlepoint applique.

Rare pair of shoes made in 1780.

A bisque headed character doll by Simon & Halbig.

Bisque headed doll with composition body and limbs stamped Thuringa, Germany.

German doll made by Herm. Steiner, 1912, 16in. long.

Armand Marseille bisque headed doll, 17in. high.

Jumeau bisque doll impressed Paris Fr.A.7, 15in. high.

A bisque headed child doll with jointed composition body, marked S.F.B.J. Paris 10, 23½in. tall.

French bisque Bru doll with paperweight eyes and kid body, 22in. tall.

Victorian doll impressed 'Fabrication Francaise al and Cie Limoges Cherie 5' 19in. high.

20th century bisque headed Googly doll by Simon and Halbig.

Simon & Halbig Japanese character doll.

American Ives & Co. clockwork walking doll, circa 1880, 9½in. high.

A George II painted wood doll, the face partly repainted and fingers damaged, 22in. high.

Parian doll with cloth body, 14in. tall.

Kammer & Reinhardt celluloid character doll.

Bisque headed Bebe doll by Bru, Paris, 24in. high.

Jumeau phonograph doll.

Small Victorian doll's house with a hinged front, 14in. high.

A doll's wooden house in the form of a three-storey building, with nine rooms.

A large, painted, doll's wooden house, the lower section with outside staircase, 5ft.2in. high, 4ft. wide.

Victorian doll's house, 2ft. 4in. high.

Rare Regency painted wooden two-storey doll's house and stand, 3ft.1in. wide.

A mid Victorian three-storey doll's house on stand, 3ft.5in. wide.

Victorian doll's house, completely fitted with furniture.

Fine mid Victorian doll's house, fully furnished, 3ft. 9in. wide.

ENAMEL

Bilston spaniel bon-bonniere, circa 1770-75, 5cm. wide.

Liberty & Co., silver and enamel frame, 29cm. high, Birmingham, 1905.

German enamel snuff box, circa 1757, 3¼in. wide.

Russian enameled egg with pull-off top by Pavel Ovtschinnikov, Moscow, circa 1900.

French enameled brush **set, mirror, 24.25cm. high, maker's mark 'JM', 1930's.**

Large pair of French or Swiss enameled opera glasses, 11.5cm. high, circa 1875.

17th century Limoges enamel hexalobate dish by Jacques Laudin, 6½in. wide.

Late 19th century Viennese enamel nef with gilt metal mounts, 14cm. high.

Chelsea etui of cylindrical form, circa 1756.

Mid 18th century jasper and gold mounted etui.

George II etui, circa 1745, in green shagreen case.

Gilt metal etui on a chatelaine with dark and light brown agate pendants.

A rare 'Girl in a Swing' etui with Columbine head top, circa 1754.

Continental gilt metal etui with some fittings.

Unusual silver etui, probably English, circa 1770, 10.5cm. long.

Gold mounted shagreen and enamel etui, late 18th century, Swiss, 4in. high.

An etui depicting a girl holding a basket, circa 1756.

Bilston enamel rainbow etui case, 4½in. high, circa 1765-70.

FANS

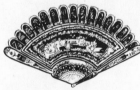

Fan with collection of forty signatures of composers, authors, etc., 1895.

Early 19th century Chinese lacquer brise fan, black sticks painted in shades of blue, red and green. 20cm. long.

Faberge lace fan with blond tortoiseshell sticks.

Victorian lace fan with embroidered flowers.

Lace fan with mother-of-pearl sticks, circa 1890, 27cm. long.

French fan set with mother-of-pearl panels, circa 1760, 10in.

ARMOIRES

Early 18th century Anglo-Dutch walnut armoire, 65in. wide.

17th century Dutch oak armoire, 220cm. wide.

Mid 18th century Dutch walnut armoire, 67½in. wide.

Good late Louis XV provincial Bas'Armoire, circa 1765, 4ft.2in. wide.

Early 17th century North German fruitwood and oak armoire.

Mid 18th century Louis XV walnut Provincial armoire, 4ft.9in. wide.

Late 16th century Flemish walnut armoire, 5ft.6in. wide.

19th century Dutch mahogany and marquetry armoire.

Dutch walnut and marquetry armoire with arched molded cornice, 74in. wide.

Late 18th century North German or Scandinavian elm armoire, 84in. wide.

Late 17th century Italian walnut armoire with carved frieze, 46in. wide.

South German armoire.

18th century Spanish oak armoire with doors centered by roundels, 55½in. wide.

Mid 18th century French Provincial oak armoire, 172cm. wide.

Late 18th century French Provincial walnut armoire, 4ft. 10in. wide.

18th century French armoire in oak veneered with tortoiseshell, 1.47m. wide.

BEDS

Chippendale mahogany low-post bedstead, 52in. wide.

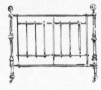

Mahogany and burl walnut double bed by Louis Majorelle, circa 1897, 68½in. wide.

Brass half-tester bed, circa 1900, 76in. wide.

Walnut half-tester bed, circa 1900, 83 x 58¼in.

Mid 20th century softwood and simulated bamboo tester bed, 72¾in. long.

One of a pair of Biedermeier beds in golden burr and straight cut elm, 6ft.5in. long, circa 1840.

Victorian mahogany bed with quilted headboard.

Part of a neo-Gothic suite of bedroom furniture.

George III four-poster bed.

Louis XVI carved walnut bed, 3ft.7½in. wide, circa 1790.

Victorian mahogany double bunk set.

Italian painted pinewood bed, 4ft.8in. wide, circa 1690.

Jacobean four-poster bed with hangings.

Unusual Regency mahogany folding campaign bed, 7ft. 4in. high.

18th century French bed, circa 1780, with shaped ends, canopy and bedspread, 8ft. 6in. high.

17th century tester bed with contemporary crewel work hangings.

BOOKCASES

A walnut square revolving bookcase, with pierced brass gallery, 3ft. high.

Early 19th century Regency mahogany revolving bookstand, 53in. high.

Late 19th century oak hanging bookcase with glazed doors, 3ft.8in. wide.

George III mahogany bookshelves supported on a central column with quadruple splayed feet.

A tortoiseshell bamboo bookcase with glazed doors.

Victorian pinewood bookshelves, 3ft. wide.

William IV pedestal bookcase in rosewood, 19½in. high.

19th century walnut open bookshelves with white marble top.

Ebonised and gilt bookcase, circa 1870.

George III breakfront mahogany library bookcase.

Late 18th century mahogany bookcase in the Chippendale style.

Breakfront mahogany bookcase with marquetry motifs on cornice, 9ft. high.

George IV library bookcase, circa 1825, 6ft.2in. wide.

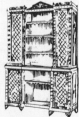

Regency mahogany bookcase by G. Oakley, 78½in. wide.

Oak bookcase with glazed upper half and carved doors.

19th century mahogany bookcase, 5ft.8in. wide.

FURNITURE

BUREAUX

Heavily carved Victorian oak bureau of four long graduated drawers with lion mask handles, 3ft. wide.

19th century Oriental carved teak bureau.

An Edwardian mahogany inlaid bureau with satinwood banded borders and four long drawers, on bracket feet, 2ft.6in. wide.

20th century oak bureau with oxidized handles.

Georgian mahogany bureau of good color, 3ft. wide.

Rosewood and marquetry French bureau de dame, circa 1870, 65cm. wide.

An attractive bureau in golden ash crossbanded in walnut with a fine patina, 36in. wide, 41in. high, 20in. deep, circa 1740.

Louis XV Provincial walnut bureau, circa 1750, 3ft.7in. wide.

Louis XV secretaire by Bernard II Van Risen Burgh, 26½in. wide.

English Queen Anne period oak bureau veneered with walnut, 94cm. wide.

North Italian walnut marquetry and parquetry bureau with fitted interior.

Early George III mahogany bureau on stand, 3ft. wide.

South German walnut bureau with inverted serpentine lower part, circa 1750, 3ft. 4in. wide.

Late 18th century Dutch mahogany cylinder bureau.

18th century Dutch marquetry double bureau, 4ft. 9in. wide.

Italian walnut marquetry bureau, circa 1780, 4ft.1in. wide.

BUREAU BOOKCASES

20th century oak bureau bookcase with H stretcher.

18th century German walnut bureau cabinet.

Edwardian mahogany bureau bookcase on cabriole legs.

George I red japanned bureau cabinet, 3ft.4in. wide.

George III mahogany cylinder bureau bookcase, circa 1780, 3ft.8in. wide.

Victorian bureau bookcase with glazed upper half.

Oak cylinder bureau cabinet, possibly German, circa 1780, 4ft.1in. wide.

Mid 18th century walnut and floral marquetry bureau cabinet.

Mid 18th century Sicilian bureau cabinet in walnut and marquetry, 1.07m. wide.

George III mahogany bureau bookcase, 3ft. 11in. wide.

A 19th century floral marquetry bureau bookcase on cabriole legs.

Georgian mahogany bureau cabinet.

Late 19th century satinwood bureau cabinet, 24½in. wide.

Dutch mahogany cylinder bureau bookcase.

Walnut bureau cabinet, circa 1715, with mirrors on the outside of the doors, 47½in. wide.

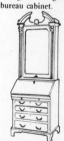

George I walnut bureau bookcase with broken circular pediment.

CABINETS

George III satinwood side cabinet, 3ft.2in. wide, circa 1770.

Mid 19th century mahogany side cabinet, 40in. wide, with hinged top.

Late 19th century carved oak coal cabinet with brass handles.

William and Mary seaweed marquetry cabinet on stand.

Edwardian rosewood music cabinet with a fall front and glazed door.

Art Nouveau style beechwood music cabinet.

17th century Austrian marquetry cabinet on stand, 31in. wide.

Charles II black and gold lacquer cabinet on stand, 50in. wide.

George III mahogany cabinet on stand with marquetry panels on the doors.

Fruitwood marquetry display cabinet, by Majorelle, circa 1910, 64cm. wide.

Bronze mounted Louis Philippe inlaid whatnot-cabinet.

17th century German carved walnut cabinet, 64in. wide.

17th century Italian walnut cabinet, 63½in. wide.

Walnut dental cabinet, circa 1890, figured in burr-wood, 29¼in. wide.

Fine Oriental hardwood cabinet, gold panels with ivory carvings, 48in. wide.

Partly 17th century Dutch oak cabinet, 64in. wide.

CANTERBURYS

Early 19th century mahogany music canterbury on short turned legs.

Early 19th century William IV rosewood canterbury, 20in. wide.

Burr-walnut music canterbury with nicely shaped partitions.

Reproduction mahogany, flat splat canterbury.

Victorian ebonized canterbury on short turned legs.

George III mahogany canterbury with flat splats.

Victorian mahogany canterbury with fret cut partitions.

Victorian rosewood canterbury with a drawer below.

Early 19th century Regency black-painted and gilded canterbury, 23in. wide.

Late George III mahogany plate canterbury, 1ft. 9in. long, circa 1805.

George III mahogany canterbury on slender turned tapered legs.

Regency rosewood canterbury with drawer, 48cm. wide.

Mid Victorian walnut stand with canterbury below, 2ft. 6in. wide.

Victorian burr-walnut music canterbury with fretted partitions and drawer in the base.

Mid 19th century walnut canterbury, top tier with fretwork pierced gallery, 25in. wide.

Victorian bamboo canterbury with lacquered panels.

DINING CHAIRS

One of two rush-seated spindleback dining chairs.

One of a pair of Art Deco giltwood chairs, 94cm. high.

19th century child's chair in elm.

One of a set of six mahogany dining chairs, circa 1840.

One of a set of six chairs, by Thompson of Kilburn.

One of a set of six English rosewood drawingroom chairs, circa 1860.

One of a set of seven George III mahogany dining chairs.

19th century Continental carved teak chair on paw feet.

One of a pair of oak chairs, by Charles Rennie Mackintosh, circa 1900, 112cm. high.

One of a set of six painted and giltwood chairs, late 19th century, partly upholstered in petit point.

Late 18th century carved mahogany Chippendale style dining chair.

One of a set of six William IV dining chairs.

One of a set of seven Regency beechwood chairs, with an X-shaped splat.

One of a set of seven Dutch walnut marquetry chairs, mid 18th century.

One of a set of eight Regency ebonized and gilded dining chairs.

Queen Anne solid walnut single chair, circa 1710.

EASY CHAIRS

Victorian oak rocking chair.

Gustav Stickley oak Morris chair with slanted arms, New York, circa 1906, 33in. wide.

Late Victorian oak easy chair with padded arms.

One of a pair of Victorian mahogany tub chairs on cabriole legs.

Large Art Deco giltwood tub chair, early 1920's.

Mahogany armchair, 1860's, on cabriole legs with castors.

Mid Victorian rosewood armchair.

Beechwood armchair, circa 1680, with padded back and seat.

George III mahogany chair, circa 1775.

Late Victorian easy chair.

Regency mahogany bergere, circa 1810.

A Victorian waxed rosewood spoon back easy chair on turned legs.

Fine George III mahogany saddle wing chair, 81cm. wide.

Fine Charles II giltwood armchair, on paw feet.

19th century highly carved hardwood easy chair.

George III mahogany library armchair of Chippendale style, arm supports carved with foliage.

ELBOW CHAIRS

Comb back Windsor armchair.

Victorian elm smoker's chair.

One of a set of eight George III mahogany dining chairs, circa 1780.

Late 19th century Japanese carved oak armchair with serpentine cloud form apron, 34½in. high.

George III mahogany armchair, circa 1785.

One of a set of eight early George III mahogany ladderback chairs, circa 1765.

One of a pair of George III giltwood open armchairs with rounded arched backs.

Queen Anne walnut armchair with solid vase-shaped splat and needlework seat.

One of a set of eleven George III mahogany dining chairs.

George III mahogany armchair, circa 1770.

One of a set of eight mid 18th century Dutch marquetry chairs.

One of a pair of heavily carved oak chairs.

One of a pair of George III mahogany armchairs, circa 1765.

Yew-wood high back Windsor elbow chair.

18th century mahogany lattice back armchair, with upholstered seat.

Charles II open armchair, 1662, with curved arms.

CHESTS OF DRAWERS

English oak chest of drawers, 39in. wide, circa 1930.

An Edwardian walnut chest of drawers with pierced brass handles.

Early 19th century Empire style chest with a figured marble top.

George III mahogany chest of three drawers, 92cm. wide.

Victorian figured mahogany bow-fronted chest on bun feet, 3ft.6in. wide.

Victorian Wellington chest veneered in rose-wood.

19th century walnut military chest of drawers, 99cm. wide.

George II mahogany linen press and chest, 3ft.1in. wide, circa 1760.

Late 16th century Italian walnut chest, 3ft.8in. wide.

French Provincial walnut veneered chest of drawers, Charles X period, circa 1820.

Dutch marquetry and mahogany chest.

Jacobean oak chest with a pair of geometrically molded doors, 3ft.3in. wide.

George II mahogany bachelor's chest, circa 1740, 3ft. wide.

Dutch marquetry chest of drawers, circa 1760, 3ft.1in. wide.

Small George III serpentine fronted mahogany chest, 3ft.3in. wide, circa 1785.

William and Mary marquetry chest of drawers.

CHESTS ON CHESTS

Early Victorian mahogany chest on chest with boxwood string inlay and pressed brass handles.

George III mahogany tallboy on ogee feet with an arched pediment.

17th century oak chest in two sections, decorated all over, 38in. wide.

A fine quality 18th century walnut tallboy with fluted pilasters and a shaped apron.

George III mahogany bow-fronted tallboy, 104cm. wide.

Late 18th century oak chest on chest.

18th century Queen Anne burr-walnut cabinet on chest, 109cm. wide.

George I walnut tallboy, base with secretaire drawer, 42½in. wide.

Late 18th century flame mahogany chest on chest on ogee feet.

18th century walnut tallboy chest on bun feet.

Late 18th century bow-fronted mahogany chest on chest on splayed feet.

Late 18th century mahogany chest on chest with a secretaire drawer.

19th century figured mahogany tallboy, 42in. high.

18th century mahogany chest on chest fitted with brushing slide.

George III oak tallboy, circa 1780, 3ft.10in. wide.

Late 18th century Irish mahogany tallboy on claw feet.

CHESTS ON STANDS

Chippendale walnut chest on stand, 42in. wide, circa 1760.

William and Mary chest on stand, 3ft.5in. wide, circa 1690.

Late 17th century Flemish ebonized and decorated chest on stand.

Early 18th century chest on stand in oyster walnut veneer inlaid with floral marquetry.

George I walnut chest on stand, 3ft.3in. wide, circa 1720.

William and Mary oyster veneered walnut cabinet on stand, 3ft.2in. wide, circa 1695.

Early 18th century walnut chest on stand.

A Queen Anne mulberry wood chest on stand with onion shaped feet.

Early 18th century walnut chest on stand.

Walnut chest on stand, circa 1710, 3ft.7in. wide.

George III oak chest on stand.

George I oak and walnut tallboy on cabriole legs.

Portuguese rosewood chest on stand, 40¾in. wide.

Small oak chest on stand with molded drawer fronts, 52in. high, circa 1780.

A fine William and Mary oyster veneered cabinet on stand with barley twist legs and cross stretchers.

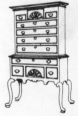

American fruitwood highboy on cabriole legs.

CHIFFONIERS

Early 19th century figured mahogany chiffonier with paneled doors.

Fine quality rosewood chiffonier, 45in. wide.

Late 19th century oak cupboard.

Victorian mahogany chiffonier with arched panel doors.

William IV rosewood side cabinet, 5ft.6in. wide, circa 1835.

Edwardian walnut chiffonier with carved cupboard doors.

Early 19th century rosewood chiffonier with unusual fretted door panels, 15½in. deep, 54in. wide, 49in. tall.

Late 19th century mahogany chiffonier.

Victorian mahogany chiffonier, 3ft.1in. wide, with shelves above.

One of a pair of 19th century satinwood chiffoniers with Wedgwood jasper plaques.

Regency marquetry and brass inlaid chiffonier.

Solid satinwood chiffonier, circa 1830, 45in. long.

Regency rosewood and parcel gilt chiffonier with two shelves, 43in. wide.

Regency rosewood chiffonier with inlaid cut brass, 43in. wide.

Regency rosewood chiffonier with concave outline.

One of a pair of Regency brass inlaid rosewood chiffoniers, by Louis Gaigneur.

COFFERS & TRUNKS

18th century German oak marriage trunk, 56in. long, dated 1767.

A highly carved 19th century camphor wood chest.

Old elm chest, possibly 14th century.

17th century carved oak coffer, 120cm. wide.

Rare 17th century oak domed top ark of plank construction, 97cm. wide.

George II walnut and mahogany chest with hinged lid, circa 1740, 3ft.9in. wide.

17th century oak and yew small coffer on gothic arcaded trestle supports, 30in. wide.

George II black japanned chest, mid 18th century, with later stand, 4ft. 1½in. wide.

Dutch colonial nadun wood chest, 40in. wide

18th century Indian Indo-Portuguese blanket chest, heavily carved, 58in. long.

17th century Spanish iron chest, 31in. wide, with floral painted panels.

Late 19th century walnut coffer.

Late 18th century dark green leather hide covered coaching trunk, 36in. long.

Late 15th century Piedmontese walnut cassone, 4ft.8in. wide.

Late 18th century pine coffer on bracket feet.

COMMODE CHESTS

18th century Danish walnut and parcel gilt bombe commode, 78cm. wide.

Louis XV commode in marquetry decorated with fire gilt bronze, after Duplessis Pere.

A Louis XV kingwood parquetry commode of serpentine shape with ormolu mounts.

Black lacquer and parcel gilt commode, 44in. wide.

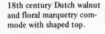

Late 18th century Italian rosewood and marquetry commode.

18th century Dutch walnut and floral marquetry commode with shaped top.

Marquetry commode with serpentine top, 46¼in. wide.

Louis XIV marquetry and ormolu mounted commode, 122cm. wide.

North Italian serpentine commode, late 18th century.

Louis XV/XVI transitional ormolu mounted marquetry commode, stamped C. Wolff.

Empire mahogany commode with black marble top, 51½in. wide.

Edwardian satinwood commode with convex center section.

Spanish mahogany commode with white marble top, circa 1825, 4ft.1in. wide.

One of a pair of Biedermeier bird's eye maple commodes, 41in. wide.

Danish walnut and giltwood commode in two parts, 4ft. 2in. wide, circa 1750.

George III satinwood and marquetry commode, 53¼in. wide.

COMMODES & POT CUPBOARDS

Early 19th century mahogany night commode, 25½in. wide.

19th century French walnut pot cupboard on shaped legs.

French Directoire bidet with marble top, 52cm wide.

Victorian mahogany one step commode on short turned legs.

Victorian bamboo and cane pot cupboard.

Victorian mahogany commode complete with liner.

Edwardian inlaid mahogany bedside cupboard.

George IV mahogany bedside commode with fall front, 67cm.

19th century mahogany inlaid commode with cupboard and drawers, 1ft.11in. wide.

Late 18th century satinwood bedside table on square tapering legs.

A George III mahogany tray top commode with sliding drawer.

A fine early 19th century traveling commode with sunken brass carrying handles and a Spode basin.

18th century marquetry bedside cupboard, 2ft.6in. high.

19th century mahogany lift-up commode with ebony inlay.

Victorian mahogany pot cupboard with fluted sides.

Late 18th century Chippendale style mahogany night table, 23in. wide, with tray top.

CORNER CUPBOARDS

Late 18th century pine corner cupboard of good color.

George III walnut veneered corner cupboard with swan neck pediment.

19th century carved oak corner cupboard.

George I black lacquer hanging corner cabinet, 36½in. high.

Late 18th century mahogany hanging corner cupboard.

One of a pair of late 18th century mahogany cabinets with shaped marble tops.

A mahogany wall corner cupboard, with swan neck pediment and dentil cornice above trellis glazed door, 2ft.6in. wide.

One of a pair of mid 18th century Louis XV ormolu mounted kingwood parquetry encoignures, 3ft.0½in. high.

Carved and painted corner cupboard with pierced cornice, circa 1760, 2ft. 5in. wide.

George III stripped pine corner cupboard with shaped shelves.

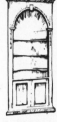

Georgian domed corner cupboard, circa 1740.

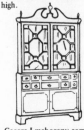

George I mahogany corner cupboard, 4ft. wide.

Edwardian mahogany corner cabinet, 40in. wide.

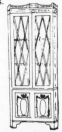

Late 18th century inlaid mahogany corner cupboard.

Georgian mahogany corner display cabinet, 3ft.6in. wide.

18th century Dutch marquetry corner cupboard.

COURT CUPBOARDS

Mid 17th century oak court cupboard with carved frieze, 4ft.6in. wide.

Mid 19th century oak court cupboard, 51in. wide.

Stained oak court cupboard, made in the mid 19th century.

Commonwealth oak court cupboard with molded cornice, 67in. wide.

17th century oak court cupboard, 61in. wide.

Late 17th century Welsh oak duodarn, 48in. wide.

Commonwealth oak court cupboard with molded rectangular top, 44½in. wide, inlaid with bone and mother-of-pearl.

Late 17th century Welsh oak court cupboard.

Queen Anne oak court cupboard, circa 1710, 4ft.3in. wide.

Bleached oak court cupboard, 57in. wide, circa 1860.

Charles I oak court cupboard, circa 1630, 3ft. 8½in. wide.

Continental oak court cupboard, heavily carved and of good size.

17th century French oak dressoire with geometric inlay and blind fret decoration, 52in. wide.

18th century oak court cupboard with fielded panels.

20th century Jacobean style oak court cupboard.

Continental court cupboard with fitted drawer and under tray.

FURNITURE

CRADLES

Victorian wickerwork cradle.

A Normandy carved oak cradle with openwork end bobbin panels, 3ft.4in. wide.

Dutch child's cradle in the form of a sledge, 22in. long.

19th century Breton style cradle, with turned finials, 90cm. wide.

Late 18th century mahogany crib.

Oak cradle with carved lunettes and lozenge decoration.

A 19th century painted wood boat cradle.

George IV mahogany cradle, 3ft.1in. wide, circa 1825.

Victorian cast iron cradle on castors.

19th century mahogany crib with carved end, 97cm. long.

17th century Continental oak crib.

A 19th century Indian cradle.

Early 19th century pinewood cradle on rockers, 36in. long.

Regency caned mahogany cradle, 3ft.11in. high, circa 1820.

17th century oak cradle with pointed hood, 3ft. long.

Mid 19th century painted cradle, 38½in. long.

Kidney-shaped Empire style child's cradle, circa 1800, 39in. long.

Early 17th century hooded oak baby's cradle.

A Victorian brass crib.

Early 19th century parcel gilt mahogany cradle, 3ft.11in. wide.

CREDENZAS

Walnut side cabinet, circa 1870, 4ft.9in. wide.

A fine Victorian walnut credenza, with shaped ends and ormolu mounts

Victorian walnut credenza with concave ends and a glazed center door.

Marquetry kingwood porcelain mounted side cabinet, circa 1870, 82in. wide.

Italian Renaissance walnut credenza, circa 1580, 4ft. 9½in. wide.

19th century rosewood breakfront credenza.

19th century French red Buhl breakfront cabinet, 6ft. 9in. wide.

Italian walnut credenza on plinth base, 45in. wide.

Ebonised porcelain and gilt bronze mounted display cabinet, 1860's, 72in. wide.

Good walnut side cabinet, 1880's, 76in. wide.

Mid 19th century walnut side cabinet, 67in. wide.

Victorian burr-walnut breakfront credenza with canted corners, 5ft.7in. wide.

French ebonized and inlaid breakfront three door dwarf cabinet decorated with Sevres type oval figure scene, porcelain plaques and ormolu mounts, 60 ins. long

Mid 19th century walnut credenza with marquetry designs.

Good burr-walnut side cabinet, 1860's, 72in. wide.

CUPBOARDS

Charles I oak food cupboard.

18th century Continental carved walnut bread cupboard with spindled front.

Late Victorian carved oak buffet.

Regency walnut cupboard with molded top, circa 1730, 4ft. 7in. wide.

Mid 17th century oak cupboard, 4ft.1in. wide.

'Mouseman' oak cupboard, 36in. wide, circa 1936-40.

Late 19th century oak side table with cupboard.

18th century Normandy Regency bridal cupboard in oak.

George III mahogany clothes press, 51in. wide.

Mid 19th century carved oak cupboard, 145cm. wide.

Swiss pewter-inlaid walnut standing cupboard, circa 1700, 1ft.9½in. wide.

German walnut parquetry cupboard, circa 1740, 6ft. 2in. wide.

Fine Art Nouveau mahogany sideboard cupboard, French, circa 1900, 59in. wide.

Mid 18th century Dutch marquetry cupboard, 5ft.8in. wide.

17th century Flemish oak cupboard, 68¾in. wide.

18th century oak settle with paneled cupboard doors.

DAVENPORTS

Mid 19th century walnut Davenport, 32 x 23½in.

Walnut harlequin Davenport, 1860's, 23in. wide.

Victorian rosewood Davenport, 53cm. wide.

Mid 19th century walnut Davenport, 21¼in. wide.

Late 19th century walnut Davenport, 24in. wide.

Attractive George III mahogany Davenport.

Unusual walnut Davenport writing table, circa 1870, 20¾in. wide.

Walnut harlequin Davenport, circa 1860, 23in. wide.

Burr-walnut inlaid ebonized Davenport, 22in. wide, circa 1860-80.

Victorian burr-walnut piano top Davenport desk.

Walnut Davenport, circa 1860, 37½in. wide, with central turned balustrade.

Walnut and burr-walnut Davenport, 1870's.

Satinwood crossbanded mahogany Davenport, 1ft. 9in. wide, 1900's.

William IV rosewood Davenport, circa 1830, 1ft.9in. wide.

Oak Davenport with three quarter gallery, 1880's, 24in. wide.

Regency rosewood Davenport surmounted by a brass gallery, 17in. wide.

DISPLAY CABINETS

19th century burr-walnut display cabinet with brass escutcheons.

19th century heart-shaped specimen table, inlaid with marquetry.

19th century mahogany specimen table on cabriole legs with ormolu mounts.

Two-tier glazed display cabinet, on cabriole legs.

Early display cabinet, by Charles Rennie Mackintosh, circa 1895.

An Edwardian mahogany display cabinet, with mirror backed central and lower scroll backed glazed side cupboards.

Chippendale mahogany display cabinet with a blind fret cornice, 57in. wide, circa 1890.

Early George III mahogany display cabinet, 4ft. wide.

19th century Chinese hardwood display cabinet.

French 'Vernis Martin' vitrine decorated by Paeli.

Fine quality 19th century carved mahogany display cabinet.

Mahogany vitrine, circa 1895, 68in. high.

Louis XV silver display cabinet with gilt bronze mounts.

Finely carved late 18th century Oriental hardwood display cabinet.

Walnut and parcel gilt cabinet on stand with glazed top, 40in. wide.

Early 18th century Dutch mahogany and marquetry display cabinet, 5ft.6in. wide.

DRESSERS

George III oak dresser, circa 1780, 6ft.4in. wide.

Georgian oak low dresser with molded rectangular top crossbanded in mahogany, 73½in. wide.

George III oak dresser with plate racks, 5ft.7in. wide.

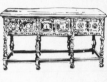

Flemish 17th century oak dresser fitted with three drawers, 7ft. long.

Early 18th century country made oak dresser, 72in. wide.

Late Georgian Welsh oak dresser, 72in. wide.

Early 20th century oak dresser with brass handles.

Late 17th century oak dresser with open shelves.

Anglesey dresser in oak banded with mahogany.

Victorian carved oak dresser with potboard.

Mid 18th century oak dresser base, 5ft.6in. wide.

18th century French Provincial oak dresser.

18th century oak clock dresser, dial signed Nathaniel Olding, Wincanton, 96in. wide.

Victorian 'Dog Kennel' dresser, circa 1850, 63in. wide.

18th century Lancashire oak and pine dresser.

Louis XV decorated cartonnier in fruitwood.

DUMB WAITERS

A small Edwardian mahogany serving table on a tripod base.

19th century two-tier dumb waiter with marquetry and ormolu mounts.

William IV period mahogany dumb waiter of three shelves, 42in. high.

George III three-tier mahogany dumb waiter on a tripod base with ball and claw feet.

HALL STANDS

Late 19th century oak hall stand with brass fittings.

Victorian mahogany hat and coat stand.

Edwardian oak hall stand.

Victorian carved oak hallstand, 7ft. high.

JARDINIERES

Mid 18th century mahogany jardiniere, 28¾in. high.

Rosewood marquetry jardiniere, circa 1900, possibly French.

19th century black lacquer and gilt jardiniere.

Mid 19th century japanned jardiniere, 2ft. 1in. wide.

LOWBOYS

Early Victorian walnut lowboy with claw and ball cabriole legs, 30in. wide.

An 18th century mahogany lowboy, 29in. wide.

Late 18th century mahogany lowboy on square cut cabriole legs.

18th century Dutch marquetry lowboy, 84cm. wide.

PEDESTAL & KNEEHOLE DESKS

One-piece mahogany pedestal writing desk, circa 1760, 81cm. wide.

Small oak kneehole desk of nine drawers, 45in. wide.

George II mahogany kneehole desk with serpentine top, 44½in. wide.

Early 20th century oak tambour top desk.

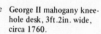

George II mahogany kneehole desk with leather lined top, 49½in. wide.

George II mahogany kneehole desk, 3ft.2in. wide, circa 1760.

19th century oak pedestal desk with tooled leather top.

Victorian mahogany cylinder top pedestal writing desk.

George IV mahogany kneehole desk, top inset with leather, 3ft.5½in. wide.

Continental kneehole desk in parquetry applied walnut, circa 1680, with hinged top, 43in. wide.

Late 19th century mahogany desk with tooled leather top.

An unusual 18th century walnut kneehole desk on bracket feet.

George II padoukwood kneehole writing table with leather writing surface, 2ft.11½in. wide.

Late 18th century Sheraton inlaid and decorated satinwood kneehole desk.

Late 18th century inlaid mahogany cylinder desk, 44in. wide.

William and Mary period walnut kneehole desk with ebony arabesque marquetry inlay.

SCREENS

American leaded glass firescreen, circa 1900, 45¼in. high.

Early 20th century ebonized and giltwood three-fold screen.

Early 20th century oak firescreen.

Three-fold painted screen, circa 1910, panel signed Jules Vernon-Fair.

John Pearson bronze and wrought iron firescreen, circa 1906, 27½in. high.

Late 18th century giltwood firescreen with needlework panel.

Early 19th century six-leaf screen, 70½in. high.

Mahogany pole screen on tripod supports with tapestry in rococo frame.

Giltwood and stained glass screen, circa 1900, 62in. wide.

Mahogany and leather five-fold screen, circa 1900, 85in. wide overall.

Late 19th century brass and glass firescreen.

Jennens and Bettridge papier mache firescreen, 41in. high, circa 1850.

Japanese ivory table screen, 12½in. high.

Louis XVI giltwood screen with eight panels.

Lacquer paneled two-fold screen with carved ivory ornamentation.

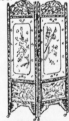

Late 19th century hardwood four-fold screen, 73in. high.

SECRETAIRES & ESCRITOIRES

Mahogany secretaire of the Sheraton period, interior with concave drawers and inlay, 43in. high, circa 1800.

American 'Wells Fargo' desk by Wootton & Co., 42½in. wide.

Hepplewhite mahogany secretaire inlaid with rosewood and satinwood.

Victorian rosewood secretaire Wellington chest.

Italian walnut secretaire a abattant, 2ft.9in. wide, circa 1790.

South German mahogany secretaire, 1840's, 39in. wide.

Oak secretaire, by M. H. Baillie-Scott with pewter and marquetry inlay, 46in. high.

Early 19th century Dutch mahogany secretaire.

Walnut veneered fall front cabinet of William and Mary design, 40in. wide.

Writing cabinet of dark stained wood, by Charles Rennie Mackintosh, 37¼in. wide.

Empire ormolu mounted mahogany secretaire a abattant, circa 1810, 3ft.2¼in. wide.

French secretaire a abattant in oak veneered with tulipwood and kingwood, 58cm. wide, by Jean-Francois Dubot.

16th century Spanish walnut vargueno, 4ft.2in. wide, later stand.

18th century oak fall front escritoire on chest.

Good Liege secretaire cabinet in burr-elm with ebonized and walnut banding, circa 1730, 3ft.11in. wide.

George III mahogany secretaire chest, 42in. wide.

SECRETAIRE BOOKCASES

Ebonised secretaire bookcase, circa 1880, 42¾in. wide.

Late 19th century carved mahogany secretaire bookcase with astragal glazed doors.

Empire secretaire bookcase with fold down flap.

Satinwood secretaire with scalloped gallery, circa 1900, 27½in. wide.

Unusual American mahogany secretaire, 40in. wide, circa 1860-80.

Chippendale period mahogany secretaire bookcase with ogee feet.

Late 17th century green lacquered double domed secretaire cabinet, 1.04m. wide.

Georgian secretaire cabinet, 4ft.6in. wide.

Early 18th century walnut secretaire cabinet.

Early Victorian figured mahogany breakfront secretaire bookcase, 230cm. wide.

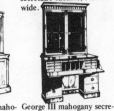

George III mahogany secretaire bookcase, 7ft.7½in. high, 4ft.1in. wide.

George III mahogany breakfront secretaire bookcase.

George III mahogany secretaire open bookcase, 81cm. wide.

Early 19th century secretaire bookcase with carved pilasters and vase shaped feet.

Queen Anne walnut secretaire cabinet, 2ft.5in. wide, circa 1710, on later bun feet.

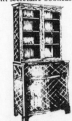

English secretaire cabinet, circa 1780, veneered with sycamore, rosewood and fruitwood, 1.2m. wide.

SETTEES & COUCHES

An early Victorian walnut framed settee.

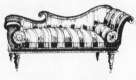

Victorian rosewood framed chaise longue on turned legs.

Edwardian inlaid mahogany settee on cabriole legs.

Victorian mahogany settee on cabriole legs, 4ft. 6in. wide

Ash settle, designed for Liberty & Co., circa 1900, 51in. wide.

Chippendale mahogany chair-back settee, circa 1880-1900, 72in. wide.

Victorian mahogany scroll end settee on turned legs.

A nicely proportioned Regency mahogany framed couch with brass inlay, splay feet and claw castors.

Victorian, rosewood, barley twist framed, couch with button backrest and turned feet with brass castors.

Louis XVI gilt canape with petal-molded frame, 4ft.5in. wide.

Oak and beaten copper inlaid settle, 1900-1910.

Louis XV beechwood canape on molded cabriole legs, 5ft.1in. wide.

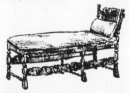

Charles II walnut day bed, circa 1660, 5ft. long with caned back.

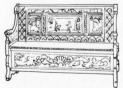

A carved oak hall settle, 56in. long.

Russian amboyna wood chaise longue with gilt enrichments.

SHELVES

One of a pair of late 19th century mahogany hanging shelves, 36¼in. wide,

19th century mahogany hanging book-shelves with ornate 'S' scroll supports.

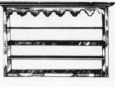

Late 18th century oak two-shelved hanging plate rack.

One of a pair of mahogany corner shelves, mid 19th century, 34in. high.

Rococo Revival walnut etagere, American, circa 1865, with pierced, carved crest, 45½in. wide.

Chippendale style mahogany wallshelves with fretted sides, circa 1760.

One of a pair of late George III giltwood eagle wall brackets, circa 1800, 1ft.3in. high.

Mahogany Regency set of hanging shelves with carved cresting, circa 1820, 26½in. wide.

STEPS

Late 18th century mahogany library steps on short turned legs.

George III mahogany library steps with brass fittings.

Set of George III folding library steps, 7ft.5½in. high, open.

George III antique oak steps, circa 1790, 17¼in. wide, original bracket feet.

Mahogany eight tread library steps with handrails, converting to a rectangular top table, on chamfered legs, 40in.

A set of early Victorian mahogany library steps which convert to a small arm elbow chair.

A set of fine Regency mahogany bed steps, 26in. high, 28in. deep, 19in. wide.

George III oak and satinwood library steps, 7ft.8in. high.

SIDEBOARDS

Large sideboard in pale walnut, 1930's, 175cm. wide.

An Edwardian bow-fronted sideboard, on cabriole legs, with a gadrooned edge.

18th century mahogany chest sideboard inlaid in the Sheraton manner.

Victorian mahogany sideboard with cellarett drawer.

George III mahogany sideboard, with reeded projecting corners and original brass knobs.

19th century painted satinwood sideboard.

George III bow-fronted sideboard.

Mid 19th century oak sideboard, heavily carved, 90in. wide.

Small 20th century Jacobean style oak sideboard.

George III satinwood breakfronted serving table, 71in. wide.

Mid 19th century rosewood sideboard, 68 x 66in.

Late 18th century padoukwood pedestal sideboard.

Early Victorian mahogany pedestal sideboard with a shaped backboard.

George III mahogany bow-front sideboard.

Attractively figured Sheraton serpentine fronted sideboard.

STOOLS

Charles II walnut stool, 3ft. 3in. wide, circa 1680.

A superb Regency stool with carved gilt rope feet.

Small Regency rosewood footstool.

Edwardian mahogany stool on tapered legs with spade feet.

James I oak joint stool, circa 1610, 1ft.6in. wide.

Victorian rosewood revolving top piano stool.

Sheraton style mahogany box strung and upholstered lyre shaped window seat.

George I walnut stool with drop-in seat, 1ft.9in. wide, circa 1720.

Second Empire mahogany stool with drop-in seat, 19½in. square, circa 1870

A mahogany inlaid oblong piano stool on square tapered legs.

Small Victorian upholstered footstool on bun feet.

20th century beech framed piano stool.

Oak stool as used by a lacemaker with under satchet for tools.

Victorian wind-up piano stool, on splay feet.

One of a pair of folding stools by Jean-Baptiste Sene, circa 1786.

An Edwardian, rush seated, oblong footstool.

Late 19th century ebonized stool on turned legs.

A Queen Anne oak close stool with simulated drawers.

A superb mid 19th century brass X frame stool, 2ft. 5in. wide.

Unusual stained walnut stool, circa 1890, 43in. high.

SUITES

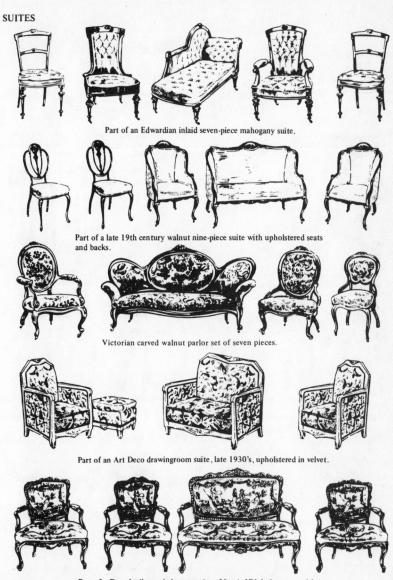

Part of an Edwardian inlaid seven-piece mahogany suite.

Part of a late 19th century walnut nine-piece suite with upholstered seats and backs.

Victorian carved walnut parlor set of seven pieces.

Part of an Art Deco drawingroom suite, late 1930's, upholstered in velvet.

Part of a French giltwood chateau suite of Louis XV design, comprising a canape, four fauteuils, banquette stool, firescreen and three-fold screen.

CARD & TEA TABLES

Victorian rosewood inlaid envelope card table with drawer and undershelf.

Regency mahogany card table.

Early Victorian serpentine front burr-walnut folding top card table.

Compact rosewood card table, circa 1860.

19th century mahogany fold-over top card table.

Late George II mahogany card table, circa 1755, 2ft. 11½in. wide.

Burr-walnut card table, 1860's, 35in. wide.

Late 17th century walnut games table with fold-over top, 33in. long.

19th century marquetry and kingwood swivel top card table.

George IV satinwood card table, circa 1825, 3ft. wide.

Rosewood card table, 1840's, 36in. wide.

Georgian mahogany card table, on cabriole legs, 2ft.4in. wide.

George II red walnut tea or games table, circa 1740, 2ft.8in. wide.

George II semi-circular mahogany card table, 1ft. 8in. wide, circa 1740.

Hepplewhite mahogany card table, 3ft. wide, on French cabriole legs.

Victorian burr-walnut folding top card table on cabriole legs.

CONSOLE TABLES

Italian painted console table on hoof feet, circa 1790.

Victorian cast iron console table with marble top.

One of a pair of 18th century gilt console tables attributed to T. Johnson.

Mid 18th century Genoese painted console table, 4ft 1in. wide.

Early 18th century George I giltwood console table, 48in. wide.

Mid 18th century German white painted and parcel gilt console table, 27½in. wide.

Early 18th century German carved oak console table.

A small mid 18th century giltwood console table with a figured marble top, 25in. wide.

Louis XV giltwood console table with brown and white marble top, 40½in. wide.

George II giltwood console table with an eagle support and figured marble top.

Giltwood console table with marble top, probably Scandinavian, circa 1770, 2ft.8in. wide.

Giltwood console table, circa 1765, by Robt. Adam.

Charles X mahogany console table, circa 1825, 4ft.4in. wide.

One of a pair of Empire ormolu mounted bronze and mahogany consoles, 1ft.6in. wide.

William IV console table in rosewood, 3ft.2in. wide.

Wood and perspex console table, 1930's, 91.25cm. high.

DINING TABLES

English walnut dining table, 60½in. diam., circa 1935.

Early Victorian marquetry center table, 64in. diam., circa 1840.

19th century oak dining table with carved frieze.

George III mahogany rent table, 42in. diam.

Regency mahogany center table, circa 1815, 4ft.1in. diam.

18th century satinwood table inlaid with bog wood.

Walnut breakfast table, circa 1860, 53½in. wide.

Mahogany octagonal breakfast table, circa 1880, with inlaid top.

19th century mahogany snap-top table on tripod base.

Regency rosewood tilt-top table inlaid with brass.

French marquetry occasional table with gilt bronze scroll feet, mid 19th century, 81.5cm. high.

Burr-walnut circular breakfast table, 1860's, 48in. diameter.

20th century oak draw-leaf table on twist supports.

Early Victorian figured mahogany breakfast table, 121cm. diam.

18th century mahogany breakfast table on reeded legs, 4ft.6in. x 3ft.4in.

Ebonized center table, circa 1870, 51in. wide.

DRESSING TABLES

Small late 18th century bow-fronted mahogany dressing table.

George III mahogany dressing table with real and dummy drawers below.

Part of a suite of Betty Joel satinwood bedroom furniture, circa 1930.

Liberty & Co. oak toilet table, 38½in. wide, circa 1900.

Georgian mahogany dressing and writing table, 36in. wide, 23in. deep, 31in. high.

Queen Anne black and gold lacquer union suite with bureau base, 21½in. wide.

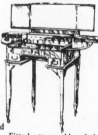

Fitted satinwood kneehole dressing table, 35in. wide.

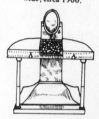

Dressing table, by Emile Jacques Ruhlmann, circa 1920, 43½in. wide.

Victorian chest of drawers with fitted top drawer, marble top and toilet mirror.

Georgian red walnut dressing table with rising top, 2ft.7in. wide.

Sheraton period mahogany 'D' table, 36in. wide, circa 1780.

A fine quality Victorian mahogany dressing table.

Louis XV kingwood and tulip-wood parquetry coiffeuse, 3ft. 1in. wide, circa 1760.

High Kitsch dressing table, 161cm. high, 1930's.

A kidney-shaped dressing table.

Bamboo and rattan dressing table, circa 1880-1900, 37in. wide.

DROP-LEAF TABLES

Regency mahogany extending dining table, circa 1815, 8ft.4in. long.

17th century Italian walnut center table.

George II mahogany drop-leaf table, 3ft. high, circa 1750.

Queen Anne mahogany drop-leaf dining table, 48in. wide.

Dutch mahogany and marquetry drop-leaf table, circa 1760, 4ft. wide.

Rare yew-wood envelope table with flap supported by a loper, circa 1730.

George III rectangular mahogany and cross-banded drop-leaf spider gateleg table.

Rare George II solid yewwood drop-leaf table with one flap. 2ft.3½in. wide. circa 1755.

19th century Cuban mahogany drop-leaf table.

Gustav Stickley oak drop-leaf table, circa 1909, 32in. diam., open.

Italian walnut drop-leaf table, circa 1610, 3ft.11½in. long.

17th century oak well table on turned legs.

George III mahogany dining table, circa 1810.

George II mahogany oval gateleg table, 104cm. wide.

Country made oak drop-leaf table, circa 1820.

Late 18th century mahogany drop-leaf dining table with six legs.

GATELEG TABLES

Mid 17th century carved oak gateleg table, 72in. wide, open.

An 18th century oak gateleg table, with turned legs.

Charles I oak gateleg table, circa 1640, 5ft.6in. extended.

A small Charles II oak gateleg table, 1ft.9in. wide.

Charles II oak gateleg table, circa 1670, 3ft.2in. wide.

Charles II large oak gateleg table, circa 1680, 5ft.10in., open.

William and Mary oak gateleg table, circa 1690, 4ft. 6in. open.

Mid 17th century oak credence table with carved frieze.

Louis XIV walnut double gateleg table, circa 1680, 4ft. 11in. open.

Rare 17th century oak gateleg table with plain gate supports, 27½in. high.

Late 17th century oak oval gateleg dining table, 4ft.8½in. opened.

Charles II oak gateleg table, 3ft.1in. wide, circa 1680.

17th century oak gateleg table, circa 1670, 26½in. diam.

A Victorian oval gateleg table, with two leaves, on turned legs, full width 3ft. 2in.

A large 18th century gateleg table with drawer, 5ft.2in. wide.

Victorian carved oak gateleg table on barley twist supports.

141

LARGE TABLES

George III mahogany three pedestal dining table, 51 x 152in. extended.

Oak dining table by J.J. Joass, 66in. long, circa 1940.

Early 18th century Continental walnut dining table on shaped legs, 6ft. long.

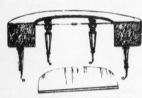

A fine, semi-circular, Irish drinking table, with additional flap.

18th century D-ended mahogany dining table.

Mid 19th century American pitch pine refectory table, 96½in. long.

George III mahogany hunting table, 8ft. 10in. long, circa 1780.

19th century mahogany extending dining table on claw and ball feet.

Solid mahogany dining table which makes two breakfast tables, circa 1830.

George III D-end mahogany dining table, 9ft. 9in. long extended.

Fine mahogany dining table with lattice underframing, George IV, circa 1825, 7ft. 6in. x 4ft. 5in.

17th century oak and beechwood center table, 83in. long.

Early 17th century oak drawleaf dining table, 133in. wide.

Late George III figured mahogany twin pedestal dining table, turned columns and splayed supports.

Single plank oak trestle-end dining table, 8ft.2in. long, with single stretcher.

OCCASIONAL TABLES

Rosewood and marquetry occasional table, late 19th century, 18¼in. wide.

Late George II mahogany tripod table, 2ft. high.

Small George II marble topped red walnut table, 1ft. 10in. wide.

Rosewood coffee table by Jacques Ruhlmann, circa 1925, 26½in. diam.

George III mahogany circular supper table, 29½in. diam.

George III mahogany architect's table, circa 1765, 2ft. 11½in. wide.

Circular Victorian table in prime condition.

A circular garden table on three cast iron legs, 2ft. diam.

George III mahogany drum top table, 3ft.7in. diam.

Solid walnut center table, **circa 1740, 2ft.9in. wide, possibly Portuguese.**

19th century Burmese carved teak wood circular table with pierced apron, 68cm. diam.

Chippendale period mahogany architect's table.

Marquetry center table, **stretchers edged with bone and ebony, 45in. wide.**

Late 18th century walnut cricket table.

Set of four marquetry tables with glass tops, circa 1900, by Galle.

Early 1920's marble topped Art Deco occasional table, 54.5cm. square.

PEMBROKE TABLES

George III satinwood 'Harlequin' Pembroke table, 36¼in. wide, open.

George III mahogany 'butterfly' shaped Pembroke table, 37½in. wide, open.

Late Victorian stripped pine Pembroke table with drawer, on turned legs.

George III faded mahogany and crossbanded rectangular Pembroke table, 77cm. wide.

George III satinwood Pembroke table, circa 1780, 2ft. 10in. wide.

George III mahogany supper table, with wire grills to the lower section, 39¾in. wide.

19th century satinwood Pembroke table, 32½in. wide.

George III mahogany 'butterfly' shaped Pembroke table, 2ft.6in. wide, circa 1780.

SIDE TABLES

Empire simulated rosewood side table, 49in. wide.

James I oak side table with bulbous supports, circa 1610.

19th century boulle side table with ormolu mounts.

Stained oak side table, circa 1880, 38in. wide.

Late 17th century oak side table, 33in. wide.

18th century giltwood side table on square tapered legs.

Fine oak side table, circa 1830, 31in. wide.

George II walnut side table, 2ft.6in. wide, circa 1730.

SOFA TABLES

Regency brass inlaid sofa table in rosewood.

Regency mahogany sofa table, 5ft. wide open, circa 1810.

Edwardian mahogany sofa table, 58in. wide.

Mahogany and marquetry sofa table, circa 1890, 44in. wide.

William IV rosewood sofa table, 88cm. wide.

Regency mahogany sofa table, circa 1815, 5ft.10in. wide.

Regency brass inlaid rosewood sofa table, circa 1815, 3ft.7in. wide.

Regency rosewood sofa table/games table with satinwood crossbanded top.

SUTHERLAND TABLES

Victorian burr-walnut Sutherland table with shaped feet.

Sutherland table in mahogany with brass inlay.

A mahogany Sutherland tea table with two folding leaves, on turned supports, 3ft. wide.

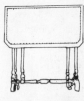

Burr-walnut Sutherland table, circa 1860, 41½in. wide.

A rosewood inlaid oblong two-tier table with folding leaves and satinwood banded borders, 2ft. wide.

Solid mahogany Sutherland table on turned legs, circa 1840.

Walnut Sutherland table, 22¼in., circa 1880.

Mahogany inlaid and satinwood banded Sutherland tea table on turned legs, 2ft. wide.

WORKBOXES & GAMES TABLES

Victorian chinoiserie lacquer work table, 28in. high.

20th century Carine parquetry games table, 37in. wide.

Rosewood work table, circa 1850, 30 x 22½in.

Victorian rosewood work table.

Victorian rosewood work table with sliding bag.

Russian ebony and boulle games table, late 18th century, 30½in. wide.

Unusual papier-mache work table with domed top, circa 1850, 19in. wide.

English walnut combined work and games table with divided swiveling top, 1850's, 28in. high.

Victorian fitted burr-walnut work table.

Sheraton period tulipwood tricoteuse of French influence, 27 x 16in.

Late 18th century mahogany games and writing table, 75 x 109 x 56cm.

Victorian rosewood needle-work table.

19th century work table with marquetry decoration, on fine turned legs.

Good quality early Victorian burr-walnut work table with a chess board top.

17th century South German games table complete with games.

Small Georgian walnut work box on square tapering legs with X-stretcher.

WRITING TABLES & DESKS

Antique mahogany architect's table with ratchet writing surface.

Art Deco galuchat and ivory, lady's writing table, circa 1930.

Late 19th century ormolu mounted kingwood bureau plat, 53in. wide.

Late 19th century oak folding desk.

Victorian pine and cast iron school desk and chair.

Edwardian inlaid rosewood writing table with inset leather top, 2ft.6in. wide.

Library table with finely marked rosewood veneers, 58in. long, circa 1840.

Edwards and Roberts fiddle-back mahogany Carlton House writing desk, circa 1900, 3ft.9in.

Queen Anne oak writing table, 31½in.

Louis XV style rosewood bonheur du jour.

Rosewood writing table, circa 1900, 32 x 24in.

Late 18th century French carved oak bonheur du jour, 40in. wide.

George III satinwood bonheur du jour on square tapering legs, 2ft.3in. wide.

Louis XIV floral marquetry bureau-plat.

Good bamboo writing desk.

Art Nouveau mahogany writing table with drawer.

FURNITURE

TEAPOYS

Victorian mahogany teapoy on a shaped platform base with scroll feet.

Regency simulated rosewood teapoy, lid inlaid with cut brass scrolling, 15in. wide.

William IV mahogany teapoy with octagonal hinged top, 14in. wide.

A Victorian mahogany teapoy on a carved base.

Regency mahogany teapoy with ebony inlay, 29½in. high, circa 1810.

George III satinwood teapoy on splay feet with brass cup castors.

Georgian period teapoy in mahogany, 20in. wide, circa 1825.

Early 19th century rosewood teapoy on platform base with vase feet.

TORCHERES

One of a pair of 18th century gilded torcheres, 45in. high.

One of a pair of oak Solomonic torcheres, 75in. high.

William and Mary walnut candle stand, late 17th century, 3ft.3in. high.

One of a pair of George III mahogany torcheres, 38¾in. high.

TOWEL RAILS

Victorian mahogany towel rail on twist supports.

Edwardian oak towel rail with spiral supports.

UMBRELLA STANDS

20th century oak hall stand.

20th century oak umbrella stand.

148

WARDROBES

Late 18th century Dutch faded mahogany wardrobe, 70in. wide.

Heal's wardrobe of 1898.

Art Nouveau style oak wardrobe with mirror door.

Victorian carved oak hall wardrobe.

A mahogany breakfront wardrobe enclosed by four panel doors, 6ft. 6in. wide.

Rare painted wardrobe by Wm. Burges, 1870's, 53in. wide.

Satinwood and painted wardrobe, 97in. wide, circa 1880-90.

Wardrobe designed by Gordon Russell, circa 1930, 72in. high.

Late George III mahogany wardrobe, 4ft. 4in. wide.

An Art Nouveau marquetry oak wardrobe, 137cm. wide.

Early 1920's walnut and ivory wardrobe, designed by Leon Jallot, 183cm. high.

Solid walnut breakfront wardrobe by Peter Waals.

Georgian period mahogany wardrobe, 48in. wide, circa 1820.

A large, good quality, Victorian pine wardrobe.

Rosewood wardrobe, by Louis Majorelle, 103in. high.

Plum Pudding mahogany gentleman's wardrobe, 54in. wide, circa 1850.

WASHSTANDS

Late 19th century walnut washstand with tiled splashback.

Victorian marble top washstand.

Victorian marble top wash stand.

Sheraton period corner toilet stand, circa 1790. 43¾in. high.

George III mahogany campaign washstand/ writing desk, 28in. wide.

George III colonial padoukwood toilet table with divided hinged top. 2ft.1in. wide.

Georgian mahogany washstand.

Sheraton period mahogany toilet stand inlaid with ebony stringing, 22in. wide.

Victorian marble topped walnut washstand.

George III mahogany square toilet stand, circa 1790, 32in. high.

Victorian marble topped washstand.

Victorian mahogany washstand on turned legs.

Regency bow-fronted toilet cabinet with divided hinged top, 3ft. 7½in. wide.

A mahogany powdering stand, with two drawers and undershelf, on cabriole legs, 3ft.10in. high.

Late 19th century marble topped mahogany washstand with satinwood inlay.

19th century marquetry corner washstand.

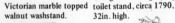

WHATNOTS

Oriental three-tier hardwood display stand.

William IV rosewood whatnot with barley twist supports.

Regency whatnot with two drawers, 26½in. wide, 15in. deep, 29½in. high.

Late 19th century oak whatnot.

Carved oak square four tier whatnot with drawer in base, 1ft. 8ins.

Victorian walnut whatnot of serpentine form.

Mahogany whatnot, 1840's, 55½in. x 21in.

A Victorian walnut serpentine front three-tier whatnot with a drawer in the base, and spiral pillar supports, 1ft.11in. wide.

Victorian inlaid walnut whatnot with barley twist supports.

19th century rosewood whatnot, stenciled **Taprell Holland & Son, London**, 49cm. wide.

20th century oak serving trolley.

Regency period mahogany whatnot of kidney shape with brass string inlay and a pierced brass gallery.

Victorian inlaid walnut four-tier whatnot.

Victorian walnut rectangular three tier whatnot, 107cm. wide.

Papier mache and mother-of-pearl whatnot, 1840's, 52½in. high.

Late 17th century Japanese lacquer Shodana.

WINE COOLERS

Regency mahogany open wine cooler, 28in. wide.

William IV mahogany cellaret, circa 1820, 2ft.2in. wide.

Early 18th century Sinhalese hardwood and ebony wine cooler, 2ft.7in. wide.

Large solid rosewood Anglo-Indian wine cooler, circa 1840, 30in. wide.

George III brass bound mahogany wine cooler with twin carrying handles, 11in. wide.

Georgian dome shaped tambour shuttered wine cooler.

George IV mahogany wine cooler, circa 1820, 2ft.5in. wide.

Early George III octagonal mahogany wine cooler with brass bands.

Late 18th century Dutch marquetry oval wine cooler, 1ft.8½in. wide.

George III mahogany and brass bound octagonal wine cooler, lead lined, 17½in. wide.

George III mahogany wine cooler with brass liner and brass bound body, 23in. wide.

19th century Dutch marquetry wine cooler on cabriole legs, with brass carrying handles.

George III mahogany and brass bound wine cooler, 60cm. wide.

One of a pair of 'George III' mahogany wine coolers with hexagonal bodies, mid 19th century, 19in. wide.

Georgian oval brass bound wine cooler.

George III serpentine fronted mahongany cellarett, circa 1760, 1ft. 6in. wide.

ALE GLASSES

Unusual cut ale glass, 7in. high, circa 1770.

Balustroid engraved ale glass with slender funnel bowl, circa 1740, 18cm. high.

Opaque twist ale glass with slender ogee bowl, circa 1770, 19.5cm. high.

Dwarf ale glass, circa 1750, 4in. high, bowl with wrythen molding.

APOTHECARY BOXES

George III shagreen cased apothecary's chest, circa 1760.

Georgian mahogany and brass bound apothecary's box, complete with bottles.

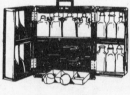

Late Georgian mahogany apothecary's cabinet, 9½in. high.

Brass bound George III mahogany apothecary's box by Cox & Robinson.

BELLS

Late 16th century silver mounted latticinio bell, 5½in. high.

Victorian cranberry glass bell, 12in. high.

BISCUIT CONTAINERS

Victorian engraved glass biscuit jar on a plated and engraved stand with bun feet.

Late 19th century glass biscuit barrel with plated mounts.

BEAKERS

Newcastle purple and white slag glass beaker.

19th century Mary Gregory beaker depicting a young girl.

North Bohemian lithyalin flared beaker by F. Egermann, circa 1830, 13.5cm. high.

Facon de Venise flared beaker, 16th/17th century, 6in. high.

BOTTLES

Sealed wine bottle of dark brown metal, 8¼in. high, 1736.

Good red overlay Pekin glass bottle, with decoration of birds in flowering prunus trees, circa 1800, 19.1cm. high.

German enameled pharmacy bottle, circa 1740, 9.5cm. high.

Bohemian Zwischengold bottle with silver cap, 12cm. high.

BOWLS

Victorian mauve carnival glass bowl.

English cut glass orange bowl, 12in. wide, circa 1790.

Miniature cameo glass bowl, circa 1880, 3.8cm. high.

19th century Lalique glass bowl of clear and opaque white glass, 10in. diam.

Early 18th century glass bowl, 11¼in. diam.

An Orrefors deep bowl by Edvin Ohrstrom, 18cm. diam.

Good Irish canoe fruit bowl, 14in. wide, circa 1810.

16th or 17th century Facon de Venise latticinio shallow bowl, possibly Venetian, 13.5cm. diam.

BOXES

CADDIES

19th century ruby glass circular box and cover, 4in.

Galle cameo glass box and cover with squat tapering body, circa 1900, 7.5cm.

Victorian purple slag glass tea caddy of sarcophagus form.

Rare Staffordshire 'enamel' tea bottle, 5½in. high, circa 1760.

CANDLESTICKS

Rare glass candlestick, circa 1710, 7½in. high.

Late 18th century free blown glass pricket candlestick, 9in. high.

Bronze and Favrile glass candlestick, by Tiffany, 8in. high.

Victorian ruby glass candlestick.

Large cut glass column with faceted stem. circa 1900, 54.5cm. high.

CANDELABRA

CARAFES

One of a pair of Lalique four-light candelabra, 9½in. high.

One of a pair of glass and gilt metal candelabra.

One of a pair of Spanish opaque white carafes, 18th century, 10¼in. high.

Ale carafe with cylindrical body and tapering neck, circa 1770, 25.5cm. high.

CAR MASCOTS

Mickey Mouse glass car mascot, stamped Walt Disney Productions, circa 1940.

Lalique glass car mascot, 1920's, 14cm. wide.

Lalique glass car mascot 'The Archer', molded in intaglio, 12.5cm. high.

Lalique frosted glass mascot, circa 1920, 17.5cm. high.

CENTERPIECES

CHAMPAGNE GLASSES

19th century cut glass and silver plated centerpiece with a glass bowl.

Large silvered metal Art Nouveau centerpiece, with a glass bowl, circa 1900, 45cm. high.

Pedestal stemmed champagne glass with double ogee bowl, circa 1745, 14.5cm. high.

Baluster champagne glass, circa 1720, 5½in. high.

CHANDELIERS

Double overlay glass chandelier by Daum Freres, 15½in. diam.

Fine glass ceiling fixture by Rene Lalique, circa 1925, 10¾in. diam.

Superb Adam style chandelier, circa 1785.

Highly colored Belgian chandelier by Muller, 61cm. high.

CLARET JUGS

Victorian silver mounted clear glass 'Lotus' claret jug, 7¼in. high, by E. H. Stockwell, London, 1880.

Victorian cut glass claret jug with silver mount, Sheffield, 1871, 28cm. high.

An exceptionally fine Webb cameo glass claret jug.

Walker and Hall silver mounted claret jug, London, 1883, 25cm. high.

CORDIAL GLASSES

Opaque twist cordial glass, with funnel bowl, circa 1765, 14.5cm. high.

A Facon de Venise cordial glass, 17th century, 4¼in. high.

George III cordial glass, with funnel bowl.

Opaque twist cordial glass with funnel bowl, circa 1765, 17cm. high.

CRUETS

George III seven-bottle cruet by William Barrett II, London, 1817-18.

George II Warwick cruet frame, Edinburgh, 1736-7, 32oz.9dwt., 8½in. high.

Electroplated eight-bottle cruet frame, mounts by Elkington & Co., 1867, 32.7cm. long.

Early George II two-bottle cruet frame by Paul de Lamerie, London, 1728, 5½in. wide, 14oz.13dwt.

GLASS

CUPS & MUGS

New England peach blown punch cup with ribbed handle, 2¼in. high.

Bottle glass beer mug with white enamel splatter.

Galle cameo glass stemmed honeycomb cup, 11.75cm. high, circa 1900.

Rare Jacobite mug, 4¾in. high, with ribbed applied handle.

DECANTER BOXES

Traveling decanter case with glasses and decanters.

'Directoire' mahogany decanter box, 19½in. high, circa 1912.

19th century rosewood traveling drinks cabinet.

Mahogany and inlaid decanter box with four cut-glass decanters, 8½in. high.

DECANTERS

19th century cut glass decanter.

Fine and very rare Giles opaque-white decanter, 11½in. high, circa 1775.

George III Waterford glass decanter, 20in. high, circa 1780.

Lalique glass decanter, 12in. high.

St. Louis decanter, 21.5cm. high, with dark blue and opaque white bands.

Victorian, green, Mary Gregory decanter.

Early 19th century ship's decanter.

Jacobite decanter, circa 1760, 10in. high.

DISHES

Webb cameo shallow circular dish, 8½in. diam.

Daum cameo glass dish, 14.5cm. wide, circa 1900.

Late 19th century gilt and enameled glass dish.

Mid 16th century Venetian gilt and enameled dish, 5¾in. diam.

DISHES, SWEETMEAT

Fine Anglo-Venetian sweetmeat dish, circa 1700, 3¼in. high.

Unusual sweetmeat dish, with cup-shaped bowl, 3¾in. high, circa 1720.

Cut glass sweetmeat glass, with double ogee bowl, 6in. high.

Sweetmeat dish with three base collars, 6¼in. high, circa 1730.

DRINKING GLASSES

Engraved composite stemmed water glass, circa 1745, 14cm. high.

18th century German Stangenglas, 8in. high.

Biedermeier drinking glass in Bristol blue and pink with etched banded panel, 6in. high.

German puzzle glass, 11in. high.

EPERGNES

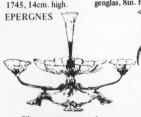

Silver epergne supporting engraved glass vase and dishes, by Elkington & Co., Birmingham, 1907, 1,457gm. of silver.

Unusual Victorian cranberry glass epergne with plated mounts, 11¾in. high.

George III four-branch epergne by Matthew Boulton, Birmingham, 1811, 8½in. high, 64oz.2dwt.

Victorian three-branch opaline glass epergne.

EWERS

A blue glass ewer ornament decorated by Mary Gregory, 43cm. high.

Central European gilt Milchglas ewer, 5½in. high, circa 1740.

Victorian cut glass ewer.

Late 16th century Venetian amethyst baluster ewer, 9½in. high.

FIGURES

Pair of figures by Lalique in frosted glass, 56cm. high.

Lalique glass bracket shelf, 1930's, 26.25cm. wide.

Rare 18th century Venetian figurine, 6in. high, in opaque white glass.

Lalique opalescent glass figure 'Suzanne au Bain', 1920's, 23cm. high.

FIRING GLASSES

Masonic firing glass of drawn trumpet shape, 3¾in. high.

Scottish Jacobite opaque twist firing glass, 3½in. high.

Color twist firing glass with small ovoid bowl, circa 1760, 4in. high.

Opaque twist firing glass set on double series twist stem, 1770, 10cm. high.

FLASKS

Colorless glass flask with spherical body, circa 3rd century A.D., 4¼in. high.

Manganese purple glass flask of cylindrical form, 3rd-4th century A.D., 4¼in. high.

Central European flask with enameled decoration, circa 1740, 17.5cm. high.

Early flattened oviform flask, circa 1690, 5½in. high.

GOBLETS

Green goblet of bright emerald color, plain stem on spirally-molded foot, circa 1760, 13.5cm. high.

Large fox-hunting goblet, 7¼in. high, circa 1760.

Baluster goblet with flared funnel bowl, circa 1700, 17.5cm. high.

Late 16th century Façon de Venise goblet, 10¼in. high, possibly Venetian.

HUMPENS

Late 19th century enameled humpen, 21.4cm. high.

17th/18th century 'Ochsenkopf' humpen with enameled body, 6in. high.

Bohemian enameled humpen, circa 1590, 11½in. high.

Franconian enameled glass betrothal humpen and cover, 1615, 41cm. high.

INKWELLS

Lalique amber glass inkwell and cover, 1920's, 15.75cm. diam.

Art Nouveau glass inkwell depicting a lizard emerging from a pond.

A Stourbridge millefiori inkwell.

A rare Tiffany inkwell depicting four frogs.

JARS

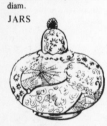

Mount Washington Royal Flemish covered jar, 7in. high.

Rare red Pekin glass covered jar, decorated in relief with a dragon among clouds, 12.5cm. high.

A large apothecary's jar, made of crude bottle glass with enamel splatter.

18th century German enameled apothecary jar, 8¾in. high.

JUGS

A Ravenscroft syllabub jug, gilt on sloping shoulders, with the label 'Honey Syllabub'.

Victorian white slag glass jug with thistle decoration.

Victorian cranberry glass jug with ridged decoration, 6½in. high.

Mary Gregory glass jug, 8in. high.

4th century A.D. pale green glass jug with strap handle, 3¾in. high.

Mid 16th century Venetian gilt and enameled jug, 8¾in. high.

Enameled Milchglas jug, **Spanish or Bohemian,** circa 1780, 19.3cm. high.

Enameled and gilt Milchglas jug and cover, 25.5cm. high, circa 1770.

LAMPS

Lalique lamp in frosted glass, 1920's, 10½in. high.

Cut glass 'Gone with the Wind' lamp, signed L. Straus & Sons, 18½in. high.

Lithophane desk lamp with five panel shade, 15in. high.

Mid 18th century French lacemaker's lamp, 25.5cm. high.

Le Verre Francais cameo glass lamp with shouldered domed shaped shade, 1920's, 40.5cm. high.

Gilt bronze and Favrile glass three-light lily table lamp by Tiffany, 13in. high.

Tiffany Studio bronze and glass table lamp, circa 1900, 63cm. high.

Tiffany spider web lamp with bronze baluster base.

GLASS

LAMP SHADES

Yellow rose bush leaded glass hanging lamp by Tiffany, 24¾in. diam.

Victorian oil lamp shade of pink glass.

Daum cameo glass lampshade, 31cm. diam, circa 1900.

19th century lithophane lamp shade on brass frame, 7¼in.

LIQUEUR SETS

Decanter and six glasses in stand, circa 1840.

Etched liqueur service in glass, 1930's.

Glass decanter and six glasses with silver mounts and silver overlay, circa 1920.

19th century Bohemian gilt drinking set, jug 33.5cm. high.

LUSTERS

One of a pair of gilt green glass lusters, circa 1850, 31cm. high.

One of a pair of Bohemian overlay glass lusters, with cranberry glass body, 25cm. high.

One of a pair of ruby glass lusters with floral decoration and cut glass drops.

One of a pair of ruby glass double lusters, about 1880.

MATCH-HOLDERS

MEAD GLASSES

Small Victorian glass boot match-holder.

A Daum match-holder of rectangular form, the pale blue frosted glass body enameled with an Alpine scene, 4cm. high.

A baluster mead glass with an incurved cup-shaped bowl, circa 1710.

Rare mead glass, 4¾in. high, circa 1700.

MISCELLANEOUS

Pair of Walter pate-de-verre bookends, 1920's, 17cm. high.

Coffee and cream glass centerpiece by Webb, 10¼in. diam.

One of a pair of glass butter coolers, covers and stands, 7in., circa 1790.

Central European opaque opaline globular teapot and cover, mid 18th century, 16cm. wide.

Large Lalique frosted glass figure of a pigeon, 14.5cm. high, 1930's.

One of a pair of large cut urns and covers, 12½in. high, circa 1790.

Rare ormolu mounted cameo glass wall flower-bowl, 13in. diam.

Pale green Roman glass vessel in the form of a bucket, 13.7cm. high.

One of a pair of St. Louis fruit door handles, 2in. diam.

One of a rare pair of 18th century enameled opaque white tureens, 4½in. high.

Pedestal stemmed stand, circa 1745, 12.5cm. high.

A Tassie glass paste portrait medallion on frosted glass over blue paper, 4¾in.

Glass vessel, possibly Roman, 2nd century A.D., 8¾in. high.

Dated St. Louis pen-holder, 1973, 13.6cm. high, set on a paperweight base.

16th century Italian verre eglomise picture, 4¼ x 3¼in.

Bohemian rose water sprinkler, circa 1850, 30.5cm. high.

GLASS

PAPERWEIGHTS

St. Louis marbrie salamander weight, 8.5cm. high.

St. Louis double clematis weight, 7.5cm. diam.

Rare New England glass fruit weight, 3½in. wide.

Clichy miniature posy weight, 1¾in. diam.

Rare, Clichy convolvulus weight, 3in. diam.

Lalique glass frog paperweight, 6.1cm. high, circa 1930.

St. Louis carpet-ground paperweight, 6cm. diam.

Rare, St. Louis magnum crown paperweight, 4in. diam.

PIPES

Nailsea pink and white pipe, 12in. long.

Rosewater pipe with wicker overlaid glass stem.

PITCHERS

Cased wheeling peach blown pitcher, 5¼in. high.

Galle carved glass pitcher in smoked glass, 1890's, 15.5cm. long.

PLAQUES

Sulphide glass cameo plaque of General Lafayette, 8.5cm. wide.

Cameo glass plaque by George Woodhall, circa 1885.

A carved cameo amber glass plaque by G. Woodhall, 16.5cm. high.

Baccarat sulphide glass cameo plaque of Charles X, 10cm. long.

GLASS

PLATES

Victorian plate commemorating Gladstone.

Venetian diamond engraved latticinio plate, late 16th century, 16.5cm. diam.

19th century light blue slag glass plate with basket weave edge.

Late Victorian frosted pressed glass plate, 8in. diameter.

POTS

A small pressed blue glass Victorian dressing table bowl and cover, 3in. diam.

Daum etched and applied cameo glass pot and cover, 12.5cm. high, circa 1910.

Lithyalin pounce-pot with pewter mount, 2¾in. high.

Unusual Pekin glass brush-pot, thinly cased in red, engraved mark of Qianlong, 17.5cm. high.

RATAFIA GLASSES

Ratafia glass with a narrow straight sided funnel bowl molded to two thirds of its height, circa 1745.

Rare Jacobite opaque twist ratafia glass with ogee bowl, circa 1765, 18cm. high.

ROEMERS

17th century Rhenish roemer of light green metal, 14cm. high.

17th century Netherlandish green tinted roemer with cup-shaped bowl, 20.5cm. high.

RUMMERS

Large engraved rummer, early 19th century, 8¼in. high.

Battle of the Boyne commemorative rummer, 1690, 6in. high.

Sunderland Bridge rummer, 6½in. high, circa 1820.

One of a pair of engraved masonic rummers, 6¼in. high, circa 1820.

SCENT BOTTLES

Guerlain 'Mitsouko' glass bottle and stopper.

Webb double overlay globular scent bottle and silver screw cover, 4in. high.

Decorated clear glass perfume bottle and stopper, 13.75cm. high.

Daum scent bottle and stopper, 5in. high, signed.

Delvaux enameled scent bottle and stopper, 1920's, 11.25cm. high.

Molded glass perfume bottle and stopper, 12cm. high, 1920's.

Rare sulphide scent bottle of flattened circular form, 7cm. diam.

Modernist glass bottle and stopper, circa 1930, 26cm. high.

SNUFF BOTTLES

Black overlay glass bottle with quartz stopper.

Chinese opaque milk-white overlay glass snuff bottle, of blue and red overlay, with agate stopper.

Chinese opaque white glass overlay snuff bottle, red overlay, with coral glass and pearl stopper.

Red overlay glass bottle with jade stopper.

Interior-painted rock crystal snuff bottle and coral stopper, 2¾in. high.

Rare enameled glass snuff bottle by Ku Yueh Hsuan.

Late 19th century interior painted glass snuff bottle.

Interior-painted snuff bottle by Ten Yu-t'ien.

TANKARDS

Central European enameled Milchglas miniature **tankard, 3¼in. high, circa 1750.**

Large glass tankard with scalloped foot, 6in. high, circa 1750.

Ruby glass tankard with silver hinged cover, 8in. high.

Central European enameled tankard and cover, **circa 1750, 24cm. high.**

TANTALUS

TAPERSTICKS

Plated tantalus frame with two decanters.

Oak decanter box, circa 1880, with Bramah lock, 13¾in. wide.

Pedestal stemmed taperstick, 5½in. high, circa 1730.

A rare taperstick, the nozzle set on inverted baluster air twist stem, 6½in. high.

TAZZAS

Venetian filigree tazza, circa 1600, 6¾in. diam.

17th century Venetian tazza, 2in. high, 6¼in. diam.

Late 16th century Facon de Venise enam- eled glass tazza, 5.9in. high.

17th century Venetian tazza, 8in. diam.

TUMBLERS

Baccarat armorial tumbler with enameled coat of arms, 9.5cm. high.

Engraved glass tumbler, 4¾in. high, circa 1790.

Venetian enameled tumbler, 18th century, 4½in. high.

Bohemian tumbler engraved with cupids and allegorial scenes, circa 1730, 10.2cm. high.

VASES

One of a pair of flower encrusted bottle vases.

18th century pale blue ground bottle vase, 8¼in. high.

One of a pair of portrait overlay green glass vases, circa 1850, 33.8cm. high.

Very rare Staffordshire opaque white enameled **glass vase, 5in. high, circa 1760.**

An escalier de cristal ormolu mounted cameo vase, 16.5cm. high.

One of a pair of Art Nouveau silver overlay blue vases.

Very rare miniature opaque white globular vase, 2½in. high, circa 1770.

Pate de verre small oviform vase, 3¼in. diam.

ARGY ROUSSEAU

BOHEMIAN

Argy Rousseau pate de cristal vase, 14.75cm. high, 1920's.

Pate de cristal Argy Rousseau vase, 10in. high.

One of a pair of Bohemian ruby overlay glass vases, 10in. high.

One of a pair of Bohemian overlay trumpet shaped vases.

DAUM

Daum etched, carved and enameled glass vase, circa 1900, 13.5cm. high.

Daum cameo glass vase of teardrop form, 30.25cm. high, circa 1900.

Signed Daum Nancy vase in orange, cream and green, 6½in. high.

Daum etched and gilt 'vase parlant', circa 1900, 26cm. high.

GALLE

Mounted Galle cameo glass vase, circa 1890's, 7.75cm. high.

Galle, etched and carved cameo glass vase, 19.5cm. high, circa 1900.

Small Galle cameo glass vase, 7.75cm. high, circa 1900.

A superb and very rare glass vase, by Emile Galle, 11¾in. high.

LALIQUE

Lalique frosted glass vase, relief molded, 1930's, 13.5cm. high.

Heavy Lalique frosted glass vase, 1930's, 25.5cm. high.

Good Lalique 'grasshopper' vase, 27cm. high, 1920's.

Heavy Lalique cylindrical glass vase, 22.5cm. high, 1920's.

LEGRAS

A Legras cameo glass vase of quatrefoil shape, the frosted glass body overlaid in purple, 13cm. high.

Legras etched and internally decorated glass vase, 39cm. high, 1920's.

LOETZ

Loetz iridescent glass vase, 18.5cm. high, circa 1900.

One of a pair of Loetz iridescent vases.

NAMED

Orrefors engraved glass vase, 18.75cm. high, 1940's.

A Brocard enamelled cylindrical vase with stylized cornflower sprays, 16.5cm. high.

Signed Sabino vase, circa 1920, with fish motif, 8in. high.

J. F. Christy oviform vase designed by Richard Redgrave, 1847, 15cm. high.

MULLER FRERES

PEKIN

Muller Freres cameo glass vase, circa 1900, 19.5cm. high.

Large Muller Freres cameo glass landscape vase, circa 1900, 55cm. high.

Pekin overlay glass vase of bottle form from the Qianlong period.

Well carved Imperial yellow Pekin glass vase of beaker form carved with blossom, 20.5cm. high.

STOURBRIDGE

TIFFANY

Late 19th century vase attributed to Joshua Hodgetts, Stourbridge, white on amethyst glass, 27.5cm. high.

Stourbridge cameo glass vase, 5in. high, central band with turquoise 'jeweling'.

Tiffany Favrile iridescent millefiori oviform vase, 6in. high.

A rare Jack-in-the-Pulpit Tiffany peacock iridescent glass vase, 1900.

WEBB

Cameo glass vase by Thos. Webb & Sons, 10.8cm. high.

Webb three color cameo glass vase.

Webb glass overlay vase amber on clear glass, signed.

Rare early 20th century Webb 'rock crystal' engraved vase by Wm. Fritsche, 25cm. high.

WINDOWS

15th century English stained glass roundel, 4½in. diam.

French stained glass panel showing the Risen Christ, dated 1542, 66 x 56cm.

Early 20th century stained glass window depicting a peacock, 22in. high.

German or Swiss stained glass panel showing a married couple, dated 1597, 33 x 24cm.

WINE GLASSES

German Royal commemorative glass, engraved with a horseman.

Fine, large gilt wine glass, circa 1760, 7½in. high.

Baluster wine glass with funnel bowl, circa 1710, 14cm. high.

Incised twist bright emerald green wine glass, 1750, 13.3cm. high.

Engraved Hanoverian wine glass, 6½in. high, circa 1740.

Facet stemmed wine glass, with ogee bowl, cut in the style of James Giles, circa 1780, 15cm. high.

Engraved color twist wine glass in the Jacobite taste, circa 1770, 14.5cm. high.

Unusual Lynn wine glass, 5¾in. high, circa 1750.

17th century Facon de Venise wine glass, 6¼in. high.

Multi-knopped air twist wine glass, circa 1750, 6¼in. high.

Very rare wine glass, circa 1740, 7½in. high.

Dutch engraved whaling glass, 7¼in. high, circa 1750.

Beilby enameled glass with **bell bowl, 6½in. high, circa 1765.**

Facon de Venise winged wine glass, Low Countries, 17th century, 18cm. high.

Canary twist wine glass with hammer molded bowl, circa 1760, 6in. high.

A magnificent Beilby armorial goblet inscribed 'W. Beilby Jr.', dated 1762, 8¾in. high.

19th century Swiss gold musical box, 2¼in. long.

George II gold five guineas young head, 1729, uncirculated.

Mid 16th century Italian gold relief of the Entombment, 2¾in. high.

Swiss gold and enamel pendant vinaigrette, circa 1830, 1¾in. long.

Gold watch key in the form of a five draw spy glass, circa 1810.

Mid 18th century shell and gold snuff box, Paris, unmarked.

Qajar gold and enamel Qalian bowl, 6.7cm.

Circular gold mounted Vernis Martin box, 3in. diameter, 1768-1775.

English gold vinaigrette, early 19th century, ¾in. high.

Faberge two color gold **engine turned box.**

Continental gold and enamel pill box.

Gold buckle by Myer Myers, New York, circa 1765.

18 carat gold presentation flask given to General Buller.

Continental gold and enamel box, mid 19th century, 2½in. long.

18th century gold brooch with ruby eyes.

Louis XVI gold-mounted mulberry composition snuff box, 3½in. diam.

Gold vinaigrette with citrine cover.

Two of a set of five 17th century gold buttons, 1¼in. long.

Mid 18th century gold box by Francois Marteau, France.

Victorian gold apple pomander with leaf ring lid, 1½in. high.

Kangxi rhinoceros horn libation cup, 4¼in. high.

One of a rare pair of hornbill skulls, 7½in. long.

18th century rhinoceros horn bowl of honey color, 18cm. wide.

Early 18th century rhinoceros horn libation cup, 3½in. high.

A fine commemorative silver-mounted horn beaker.

Carved horn, gold, enamel, and mother-of-pearl hair ornament by Lalique, circa 1900, 17.5cm. wide.

Early 19th century horn snuff mull, 5in. long.

19th century carved horn, pierced with immortals amongst trees, on rosewood stand, 74cm. wide.

Victorian brass and horn gong complete with hammer.

Good brass mounted cowhorn powder flask, 10¼in. long.

One of a fine pair of buffalo horn armchairs.

Good staghorn sashi netsuke showing Ashinaga, signed Isshin.

Tiny Ozaki Kokusai study of an owl in staghorn.

Good carved horn, enamel and moonstone hair comb, circa 1900, 13.1cm. wide.

Bohemian carved staghorn powder flask.

19th century Japanese rhinoceros horn cup with flared rim, 4in. high.

19th century three case red lacquer inro.

Early 18th century four-case inro decorated with three sages, unsigned.

Late 17th century four case inro, unsigned.

Fine 19th century Japanese five case gold lacquer inro.

19th century three-case inro of wood, carved with two panels, unsigned, sold with a wood netsuke.

Unusual two-case inro decorated with fish and waves, chipped, signed Kyukoku with kakihan.

Small 19th century inro of two cases, carved in low relief, unsigned, slightly cracked.

Single-case inro of natural wood, decorated in colored takamakie, signed Toshi.

Unusual 18th century three-case inro of gold and black lacquer, unsigned.

Two case wood inro.

Late 18th century gold lacquer inro of five cases, decorated in gold takamakie, hiramakie and kirigane, unsigned.

19th century four case inro, inlaid with pewter and aogai.

Four-case inro, signed Kajikawa saku with red pot seal.

18th century single-case inro of wide oval shape, brown-ground decorated with shell-gatherers, unsigned.

Very good five-case inro of tall shape, decorated with gold takamakie, signed Kajikawa Bunry-usai.

Small late 18th/early 19th century two-case inro decorated in pewter, unsigned.

Single valve radio, circa 1925, with original valve and tuning coil.

Barograph by Short and Mason.

18th century French brass nautical compass and folding sundial.

Brass box sextant by Elliot Bros., in drum-shaped case, 7.5cm. high.

Danish magneto desk telephone, circa 1920, 1ft.1in. high

English Imperial model 'B' typewriter, circa 1915, 1ft. wide.

Victorian cased set of scales complete with weights, 11½in. high.

Mahogany terrestrial globe by E. Stanford, dated 1878, 23in. diam.

Ship's binnacle by Hughes & Son, London, 125cm. high.

Magnificent microscope made by Alexis Magny, circa 1750, for Madame de Pompadour.

Columbia printing press, with distinctive golden eagle crest.

Late 19th century Adco false tooth vulcanizer with cast iron shell. 24¾in. high.

Brass equinoctial dial by Pizzala, London, 13.5cm. diam.

Dollond's chest type brass monocular microscope, circa 1840.

Early 19th century set of drawing instruments, 5in. long.

Unusual narrow-drum 'perfect' trout reel of aluminium and brass, marked Hardy Bros. Alnwick.

Mahogany 19th century compass.

Late 19th century American J.H. Bunnell & Co., brass recording telegraph.

Eastman Studio scale by Kodak, New York, 9in. wide.

Ferguson's terrestrial globe inscribed G. Wright, 17in. diam.

Early Culpeper microscope, 14in. high, with drawer of objectives and slides.

Unusual London Stereoscopic Co. double stereoscopic viewer, circa 1880, 1ft.8in. high.

Early 19th century George Adams waywiser, 4ft.4in. high, with cast iron handles.

17th century ivory German diptych dial, dated 1650, with the trade mark of Leonhardt Mire of Nuremberg.

Unusual jockey's scale, circa 1880, with mahogany seat.

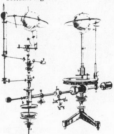

Early 20th century orrery, 3ft.5in. wide, with sectioned diagram.

Ship's Bridge Telegraph in brass, 105cm. high, signed 'Bloctube Controls'.

Marconiphone television model 705, 1940's, 36¾in. wide, in walnut veneered cabinet with hinged lid.

Good brass theodolite, 350mm. high.

Two-day marine chronometer by Breguet et Cie, dial 8cm. diam.

Late 19th century galvanometer.

Early 19th century brass theodolite of small size, by W. & S. Jones, London.

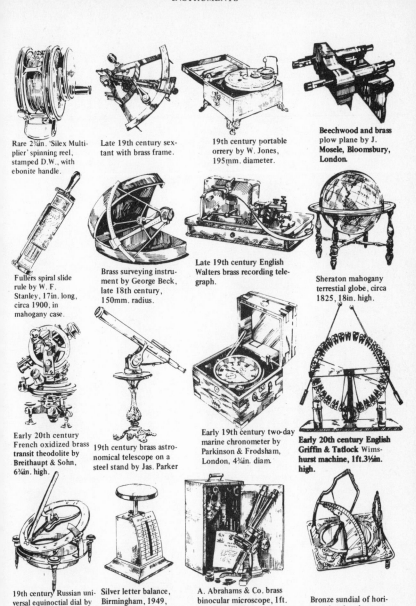

Rare 2¾in. 'Silex Multiplier' spinning reel, stamped D.W., with ebonite handle.

Late 19th century sextant with brass frame.

19th century portable orrery by W. Jones, 195mm. diameter.

Beechwood and brass plow plane by J. Mosele, Bloomsbury, London.

Fullers spiral slide rule by W. F. Stanley, 17in. long, circa 1900, in mahogany case.

Brass surveying instrument by George Beck, late 18th century, 150mm. radius.

Late 19th century English Walters brass recording telegraph.

Sheraton mahogany terrestial globe, circa 1825, 18in. high.

Early 20th century French oxidized brass transit theodolite by Breithaupt & Sohn, 6¾in. high.

19th century brass astronomical telescope on a steel stand by Jas. Parker

Early 19th century two-day marine chronometer by Parkinson & Frodsham, London, 4¼in. diam.

Early 20th century English Griffin & Tatlock Wimshurst machine, 1ft.3½in. high.

19th century Russian universal equinoctial dial by Mills of Petersberg, 9.5cm.

Silver letter balance, Birmingham, 1949, 3¼in. high.

A. Abrahams & Co. brass binocular microscope, 1ft. 6in. high, 1873.

Bronze sundial of horizontal pedestal type.

Pair of Japanese dama-scened metal stirrups.

Black-lacquered metal coal bin.

Early 18th century American wrought iron pipe kiln, 13½in. long.

Good strong iron box, circa 1670, 2ft. 8½in. wide.

Unusual painted, gilded and enameled coal container.

Wrought iron gate, 1860's, 78 x 40in.

One of a pair of mid 19th century cast iron garden urns of cam-pana form, 30in. high.

Fine cast iron figure of a classical woman, circa 1810, on 5½in. square walnut base.

Victorian cast iron footman, with shaped feet.

17th century iron strong box.

Late 19th century articulated iron cray-fish, 9in. long.

Unusual 18th or 19th century iron Buddhist traveling shrine.

Komai inlaid iron incense chest with inlaid panels, circa 1900, 8cm. high.

A large pair of 19th century sheep shears.

Early 20th century inlaid Komei iron dish showing a warrior, 8¾in. diameter

19th century Iranian steel cat with silver and gold harness.

Cast iron fronted painted wooden Mail Box, circa 1910, with brass lock, 29in. high.

Iron group of two horses by P. J. Mene, signed, 21in. long.

A pair of German iron candlesticks, circa 1910, 21cm. high.

Iron hand-held fish harpoon, circa 1720.

Iron model of a pointer after Mene, 7½in. high.

Wrought iron fire basket.

Victorian cast iron cooking pot with a medallion on the side.

One of a mid 19th century pair of cast-iron garden urns, 45¾in. high.

English cast-iron, walnut and marble occasional table with diamond registration mark for June 1845.

Victorian cast iron stove in working order.

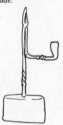

A wrought iron rushlight and candleholder on a wooden base, 17th century.

Old Islamic bottle shaped vase in steel, 8¾in. high.

One of a pair of Iranian steel doves, damascened in gold, 9½in. high.

Fireside crane with two hinges, 26½in. long, circa 1730, initialled S. W.

A large 19th century polished steel griddle.

Early 19th century steel footman, pierced with scroll and star design, 14½in. high.

Early 17th century
South German ivory
relief, 2¾in. high.

**16th century Flemish
or Northern French**
ivory Momento Mori,
2¾in. high.

One of a pair of carved
ivory sphinx candlesticks,
11½in. high, early 19th
century.

Mid 19th century French
ivory group of two chil-
dren, on gilt metal base,
9.5cm. high.

Early 18th century Italian
ivory oval plaque, 4¼in.
long.

18th century Dieppe car-
ved ivory group, 3½in. high.

**Turned ivory mortar,
6in. high, circa 1800.**

Late 19th century French
carved ivory figure of Cupid.
16cm. high.

German silver colored
metal and ivory tankard,
8½in. high.

An ivory fowl, 16.5cm.
high.

South German ivory group,
4½in. high, circa 1600.

One of a pair of early 20th
century Chinese carved
ivory goddesses, 12¼in.
high.

Late 19th century
ivory tusk vase,
25.5cm. high.

Japanese carved ivory sectional takarabune, 52cm. long.

One of a pair of Ch'ien
Lung ivory lanterns and
stands, 15¼in. high.

Attractive ivory group of
four boys, signed, circa
1880-90, 3in. high.

Ivory tankard with silver gilt mounts, 17th century, 28.5cm. high.

19th century Japanese carved ivory figure.

Mid 18th century English ivory relief, 2¾in. high.

19th century Rajasthani in ivory, 3½in. high.

Ivory figure of a young child by F. Preiss, inscribed, 9cm. high.

17th century Flemish or Dieppe ivory relief, 1¾in. high.

Japanese carved ivory group of fisherman and child, 13½in. long.

One of a pair of ivory bottles with heads as stoppers.

Good Komezawa ivory figure of Hotei, signed, 4in. high.

Carved ivory female head by Julien Dillens, 55cm. high, circa 1900.

Harpoon support in walrus ivory.

Carved ivory figure of Hsi Wang Mu, 34cm. high, Chinese, circa 1900.

17th century German ivory statuette of the infant Bacchus, 16cm. high.

Japanese ivory Okimono sectional group, signed Kyokumei, late 19th century, 7in. high.

18th century Italian carved ivory jug, 48cm. high.

Large German jeweled and ivory group of a camel led by a blackamoor, 16½in. wide.

Rare ivory bottle carved in the shape of a reclining lady.

Walther carved ivory figure of a young girl, 8.76cm. high, 1930's.

Late 19th century Japanese sectional ivory sword, 127cm. long.

Unusual Guangxu ivory acrobatic group of four articulated figures, 12.5cm. high.

Fine Nobuaki ivory group, circa 1900, 18.5cm. high.

Interesting ivory casket, partly 15th century, partly 19th century, 10in. long.

Preiss carved ivory figure of a little boy, 14.75cm. high, 1930's.

Small ivory group of Kanzan and Jittoku with good detail, signed Yoshitomo.

Early 9th century Carolingian ivory plaque from the cover of a manuscript gospel, 7½in. high.

18th century Italian ivory devotional relief, 7½in. high.

Japanese ivory figurine, 6¾in. high.

18th century ivory figure of Gama Sennin, of the Kyoto school, unsigned.

Louis XVI ivory carnet de bal.

Pair of ivory tusks decorated with mother-of-pearl, ivory and hardstone, on carved wood stands.

19th century mid European ivory tankard with silver mounts, 12½in. high.

17th century Flemish ivory crucifix figure, 16¼in. high.

Late Ch'ien Lung grayish white jade bowl, 5¾in. diam.

Mottled white and brown jade bottle.

Qianlong mottled white jade koro and cover, 6¾in. wide.

Pale gray jade hexagonal vase, 4¼in. high.

Ch'ien Lung white jade brushwasher, 5¾in. wide.

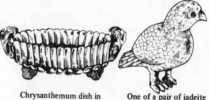

Chrysanthemum dish in dark green jade, 10in. wide.

One of a pair of jadeite parrots, 7in. long.

18th century Chinese celadon jade bowl, 23.5cm. wide.

Mottled gray and russet jade bottle with matching stopper.

Celadon jade Ting, 8¾in. high.

Ch'ien Lung grayish white jade globular jar and cover.

Fine quality 18th century jade brush washer.

Ch'ien Lung mottled white jade koro and cover, 6¾in. wide.

One of a pair of jade Phoenix.

Pale gray foliate dish in jade, 7¾in. diam.

Pale green jade figure of a lady, 12½in. high.

Cornflower blue sapphire surrounded by diamonds.

Pair of antique diamond earrings.

Platinum set single stone diamond ring, main diamond weighs 1.70 carats.

Pair of turquoise, diamond and gold stud earrings of domed form.

Mid Victorian diamond and emerald brooch.

Oval hardstone cameo, signed Verge, circa 1800, 7cm. high.

Victorian diamond and pearl brooch-pendant.

Square emerald set with diamond surrounds in 18 carat white gold.

Hexagonal silver brooch, 2.5cm. high, circa 1900.

Art Nouveau hair ornament set with rose diamonds and beryls.

Diamond three row crescent brooch, late 19th century.

Sapphire and diamond clip of miter shape, circa 1930, pierced and pave-set.

A pair of silver and enamel cufflinks, 2.25cm. high, circa 1900.

Mirror locket in Art Nouveau style in yellow gold set with turquoise matrix.

Dunand eggshell lacquer pendant panel, 13.8cm. long.

Arts and Crafts pendant possibly by Professor Joseph A. Hodel, 1.5cm. across.

Oval ruby and diamond cluster ring in white gold setting.

18ct. gold diamond cluster ring.

Victorian diamond, gold and enamel necklace.

Lady's diamond set dress ring, centre stone 1.49carat.

Jade and diamond brooch of oblong shape.

Elegant bow brooch of circular cut diamonds.

Lalique gold and enamel brooch, 3.4cm. wide, circa 1900.

Pair of antique pear shaped diamond pendant earrings.

Silver gilt and plique-a-jour enamel brooch, circa 1905, 4cm. wide.

Fine antique diamond pendant surmounted by a ribbon bow on chain.

Gold and enamel Lalique brooch, 4cm. high, circa 1900.

Liberty & Co. plique-a-jour enamel pendant, circa 1905, 4.5cm. long.

Pearl and diamond necklace of nine strands with cannetille gold clasp.

Platinum set diamond pendant on a fine chain.

Louis XVI rose diamond and enamel necklace.

14 carat yellow gold chain, composed of alternating textured arrow and oval links, circa 1900, 22in. long.

Lalique glass lamp, 1920's, 31.25cm. high.

One of a pair of iridescent Favrile glass candle lamps, by Tiffany, 14in. high.

Modernist lamp with spherical green glass shade on blue glass base, 1930's, 31cm. high.

19th century Chinese champleve opaque enamel on bronze lamp base and shade, 20½in. high.

Spider web leaded glass, mosaic and bronze table lamp by Tiffany.

Late 19th century Burmese fairy lamp by Mt. Washington Glass Co., 6in. high.

Ship's masthead riding light in copper, 55cm. high.

Attractive Boilot bronze table lamp, circa 1900, 39.5cm. high.

Art Deco piano lamp, amber shade with floral motif supported by a bronze nude, on green marble base, circa 1925, 14½in. long.

Silvered metal Art Nouveau lamp, 40cm. high, circa 1900.

20th century American bronze table lamp in the form of a peacock, 16½in. high.

Early 20th century cut glass lamp with detachable shade.

Daum etched glass lamp on wrought iron base, shade engraved, 1920's, 50.5cm. high.

20th century millefiori lamp, 41cm. high.

Le Verre Francais cameo glass table lamp with conical shade, signed, 37.5cm. high.

Bronze and ivory lamp by Ferdinand Ligerth, circa 1910, 17¾in. high.

Austrian glass and gilt bronze lamp in the form of a peacock, circa 1920, 16in. long.

Ship's anchor riding light in copper with brass attachments, 50cm. high.

Art Deco lady lamp, 15in. high.

American half shade table lamp by Bradley & Hubbard, circa 1870, 20in. high.

Early 20th century Pairpoint bronze and reverse painted table lamp, 23in. high.

Daum glass lamp carved with marine motifs.

Spelter lamp, 16in. high, 1920's, fitted for electricity.

Bronze table lamp with pierced bowl.

Tiffany Studios 'Nautilus' gilt bronze table lamp inset with mother-of-pearl studs, 33.5cm. high.

Rare Webb's Burmese glass nightlight stand, circa 1887, 28cm. high.

Art Deco bronze lamp, 1930's, 52.75cm. high.

Doulton stoneware lampbase by Mark Marshall, dated 1882, 14½in. high.

Lacemaker's lamp with loop handle and pad foot, 23.5cm. high.

Victorian brass desk lamp with white shade.

Miniature American porcelain lamp with globe-shaped opalescent white shade, circa 1880, 9¼in. high.

Early Favrile glass and silvered bronze kerosene student lamp by Tiffany, 24in. high.

Lead band of musicians.

Late 19th century octagonal lead jardiniere cast with mice and other field animals, 21½in. diam.

Part of a set of sixteen Britain's Salvation Army figures.

Naja by Jean Dunand in patinated lead.

18th century lead cistern, dated 1764, 39in. wide.

18th century English lead figure of Christ, 124cm. high.

Set of nine lead soldiers of the band of the 1st Lifeguards.

One of a set of four mid 19th century lead garden figures, 25in. high.

One of a set of four 20th century lead peacocks, 24½in. high.

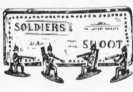

Set of four soldiers in original box.

19th century lead figure of Pan, 49in. high.

One of a set of four circular lead plaques of classical scenes, 70cm. diam.

Lead plaque of Napoleon Bonaparte on horseback, circa 1810, 9½in. high.

18th century English lead figure of a naked youth holding cymbals, 135cm. high.

One of a pair of garden urns of lead, 2ft.6in. high.

18th century English lead figure of a putto with one hand on his head, 81cm. high.

One of a pair of ormolu mounted verde antico marble urns, mid 19th century, 16½in. high.

Late 18th century neoclassic Italian marble trough, 26¾in. wide.

17th century North Italian marble negro head, 14in. high.

One of a large pair of white marble seated Buddhistic lions, 44in. high.

Marble bust of a lady by Sir John Steell, 23in. high.

One of a pair of late 17th century baroque Italian white marble seated lions, 10½in. high.

17th century Italian marble head of a satyr, 27cm. high, with two bases.

White marble group of Leda and the Swan, probably French, mid 19th century.

Black conglomerate marble head from the T'ang dynasty, 9½in. high.

16th century Italian white marble elephant, 9¾in. wide, base damaged and restored.

17th century Flemish marble figure of Venus, an urn at her side, 21in. high.

Venetian/Byzantine 14th century Verona red marble cistern, 64cm. wide.

Mid 19th century marble bust of a lady by Joseph Mitchell, 20½in. high.

Italian marble group of the Virgin and Child, circa 1400, 24½in. high.

19th century Indian marble seat, back of pointed arched form, 4ft. 3½in. wide.

Marble portrait bust of Helen Boucher, 42cm. high, circa 1930.

Rare George III satinwood toilet mirror, 1ft.5½in. wide.

Black lacquer toilet mirror with chinoiserie decoration.

Early 18th century Venetian giltwood mirror, one of a pair, 4ft.5in. high.

Tiffany Studios bronze and Favrile glass mirror, New York, circa 1920, 13in. high.

Guernardeau patinated metal Art Nouveau mirror frame, circa 1900, 41.5cm. high.

Large Art Deco mirror frame, early 1920's.

George II walnut and parcel gilt mirror, circa 1740, 2ft.7in. wide.

Early 18th century rare giltwood pier glass with divided beveled plate, 70½in. high.

Good George II parcel gilt walnut mirror, 2ft.3in. wide.

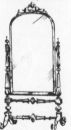

Walnut cheval mirror, 1850's, 78in. high.

Early George III giltwood mirror, 47¾in. high.

Art Nouveau bronze mirror cast with the figure of a young woman, 31cm. high.

Late 17th century Florentine giltwood mirror, 3ft.7in. high.

Good Regency giltwood convex mirror, 2ft.2in. diameter, circa 1810.

George II giltwood mirror, 2ft. 6in. wide, circa 1730.

Dresden beveled oval mirror decorated with blue and white flower spray, 10½in. high.

19th century painted wood-encased mirror, 18in. wide.

Victorian mahogany dressing table mirror.

Copper and enamel mirror, circa 1900, 40in. wide.

Toilet mirror by Gordon Russell, circa 1930, 26½in. high.

Satinwood cheval mirror, 57½in. high, circa 1900.

Koening & Lengsfeld ceramic figure of a woman looking into a mirror, 70cm. high.

One of a pair of Thuringian mirror frames, circa 1880, 99cm. high.

Sue and Mare Art Deco gilt bronze mirror frame, 1923, 25.6cm. high.

Rosewood and mahogany mirror by Louis Majorelle, 67in. high.

Italian Art Nouveau mirror with carved pearwood frame, 92½in. high.

Rare North Italian painted and giltwood mirror, 2ft.1in. wide, circa 1700.

Empire mahogany cheval mirror with arched cornice, on scrolled legs and paw feet, 78½in. high.

Chromed tubular steel cheval mirror on four castors, 1930's. 160cm. high.

William and Mary oyster veneered walnut wall mirror, 2ft. high, circa 1685.

Good Regency giltwood mirror, circa 1810, 3ft. 2in. high.

One of a pair of Chinese Chippendale giltwood miniature wall mirrors, painted with an Oriental scene.

Victorian heart shaped
pin cushion, 7in. long.

Rare George III feather
picture, 28in. x 33in.

Rare postcard
depicting a
balloon flight.

Papier mache model of
'Nipper'.

One of a pair of doors by Jean
Dunand for a Normandie liner.

One of a rare pack of
French playing cards,
about 1819.

An Indo Persian saddle
of mauve velvet covered
with gold bullion.

Pine and elm
dolly for
washing clothes.

19th century hip
bath with brass
fittings.

Stevengraph, complete
with original titled
mount 'Iroquois'.

Very fine Sand Bell,
Victorian, 9½in.
high.

Victorian black silk
parasol with embroid-
ered decoration.

17th century Venetian
sedan chair with carved
gilt wood frame and
leather panels. $1,750

Preserved human head
with tattoo ornament,
7½in. high.

Victorian carved mahogany
fire surround with mirrored
overmantel.

Stevengraph of
Victoria and her
four sons.

Early 18th century elm wheelbarrow, 22in. long.

Egyptian stucco funerary mask, about AD150-200.

Mid 19th century red boulle clock bracket, 14½in. high.

Hardstone traveling inkwell, circa 1800, 1¾in. square.

One of a pair of Rowley Gallery silvered wood doors, 1920's, 216cm. high.

Bokhara wood saddle painted in polychrome with floral and foliate designs, 16in. high.

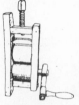

Scottish wooden miniature mangle for clerical bands.

An early oak mechanical mousetrap.

Victorian carved oak adjustable bookstand.

An unusual pair of Indian betel nut crushers.

Charles I needlework picture, 18in. wide.

Dummy board figure.

English papier mache advertising display, 36in. high, 1930's.

16th century map of the world by Ortelius.

Late 17th century Friesland octagonal foot warmer, 7½in. high.

Card from a non-standard English pack of 1679.

Bristol Crown Fire Office mark, circa 1718, lead on wooden mount, 6½in. wide.

Georgian silver lorgnette with tortoiseshell case, about 1820.

Late 18th century pair of cockfighting spurs, 1¾in. long.

Enameled silver **flint lighter, 2in. high.**

Late 18th century Spanish censer, 8½in. high, 35oz. 15dwt.

Two wax figures representing Mrs Peachum and Mrs Trapes, 1921.

Outsized English model of a Guinness bottle and glass, circa 1920.

Silver mounted tortoiseshell blotter, 13½ x 10½in., London, 1893, and paper knife, 12¾in. long.

One of a rare pair of George III silver spurs, London, 1784, maker B.C.

A Jivard shrunken head, the lips sewn with twisted fiber suspending two long plaited tassels.

Pale silk parasol, 24in. circa 1850.

Hand-in-Hand Fire And Life Insurance Society mark, in lead, 8in. wide.

Prayer book with an ivory and silver inlaid case.

Oval silhouette by Walter Jordan, circa 1788, 2in. high.

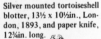

Card from an extremely rare 17th century pack of Scottish heraldry playing cards.

Good 19th century model of a coal-fired horse drawn steam fire engine, 14in. long, in a glass showcase.

Detailed 1/12 scale model of fishermen and equipment on Worthing beach, circa 1920, by S. Bunker, 29¼in. wide.

A well constructed six wheeled show-man's mobile workshop trailer, 2ft. 2in. wide.

Late 19th century model of a Lord Mayor's coach, 23in. long.

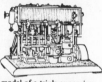

Fine model of a triple expansion marine steam engine finished in gray and mounted on a checkered base-board, 10¾in. long.

3in. scale model of a single cylinder Burrell agricultural traction engine, by K. B. Thirsk, Driffield, 1973, 45in. long.

Scale model of a Northant's spindle-sided wagon.

Well-engineered coarse scale coal-fired live steam model of a traction engine, 54cm. long.

Detailed 1/8 scale wood and metal model of a gig of circa 1850, by A. Lee, Hendon, 17½in. long.

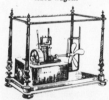

Finely engineered patent model of a twin cylinder vertical revers-ing steam plant, by W. Morrison, Saltcoats, circa 1900, 10½in. wide.

Two sections of a glass case con-taining three scenes from 'Three Little Kittens', 58in. long.

Coin-operated working model of Stephenson's 'rocket' in glass case.

Brass and copper 1/12 scale gas-fired model of a steam plant, 36in. wide.

Working model of a hand weaving loom, circa 1900, English, 2ft.1½in. high.

Model single horizontal cylinder bayonet frame mill engine by A. H. Allen, Keigh-ley, 11¼in. wide.

Tin Ocean liner, U.S. Zone Germany, circa 1947, 20in. long.

Bing tinplate gunboat with clockwork mechanism, circa 1910, 15in. long.

Shipyard model of a ship's boat with patent specification, 95cm. long.

Fine French prisoner-of-war boxwood ship model, 14in. long, circa 1800-10.

Scale radio-controled model of the salvage tug 'Lloydsman' of Hull, built by E. R. Warwick, Sevenoaks, 56in. wide.

French prisoner-of-war bone ship model, circa 1800, 10¾in. long.

Shipbuilder's detailed model of a freighter built by Wm. Doxford, Sunderland, 1947, 4ft.8in. long.

Clockwork battleship Dreadnought, 8in. long, 1920-25.

Exhibition standard boxwood and pine model of a single screw steam yacht, circa 1900, by W. Morrison, Saltcoats, 43in. long.

Fully rigged bone and mahogany model of a 16-gun Admiralty cutter, 16in. wide.

Contemporary French prisoner-of-war bone and horn model of a 112-gun man-of-war, 12in. long.

Model of the three-masted ship 'Countess Margaret', 4ft. long.

Arnold tinplate single-funneled liner in original cardboard box, circa 1925, 12¾in. long.

Fleischmann twin-funneled tinplate liner with clockwork mechanism, 12in. long, circa 1950.

Bing tinplate torpedo boat with four funnels, circa 1918, 21½in. long.

Exhibition standard 5in. gauge model of a 4-6-0 locomotive and tender 'King John', by J. Perrier, Ringwood, 73in. long.

Exhibition standard 7mm. fine scale electric model of a Webb class 1P 2-4-2 side tank locomotive, by J. S. Beeson, Ringwood, 9½in. long.

Gauge 'one' clockwork L. & N.W.R. tank locomotive by Bassett Lowke, 16¼in. long.

Early live steam locomotive, 3¼in. gauge, circa 1880.

Hornby '0' gauge clockwork train set in original cardboard box, circa 1924.

7mm. scale electric model of a condensing side tank locomotive No. 10, by B. Miller, 8¾in. long.

7mm. scale model of a London and North Eastern Railway 1st Class sleeping car, 19in. long.

Incomplete live steam model of a 3½in. gauge locomotive and tender, by Percival Marshal & Co., 3ft.10½in. long.

7mm. fine scale electric model of a 'Jinty' class 0-6-0 side tank locomotive, by J. S. Beeson, Ringwood, 9in. long.

Tinplate reversing engine 'London' by Mathias Hess, circa 1885, in original box.

Early gauge 'Three' Ernst Plank live steam boxed train set, circa 1905.

Fine early Bing gauge '0' live steam tank engine no. 3410.

5in. gauge model of the Welsh quarry 0-4-0 tank locomotive No. 1, by S. F. Price, Sheppey, 31½in. long.

3½in. gauge model of the Hunslett narrow gauge 2-6-2 side tank locomotive 'Russell', 34½in. long.

3½in. gauge display model of a Webb 2-4-0 side tank locomotive by H. A. Taylor, Bletchley, 22in. long.

German tinplate monkey money bank with decorated base, 6½in. high.

A cold painted American cast iron money box 'always did 'spise a mule', 10in. long.

Late 19th century American cast-iron negro and shack money bank, 4¼in. long.

American cast-iron Tammany money bank, circa 1880.

Late 19th century American Punch and Judy money box, 7½in. high.

One of a pair of German electroplated Britannia metal 'porker' money boxes, 13.7cm. long.

German Mickey Mouse tinplate mechanical bank, both sides having different scenes, circa 1930, 6¾in. high.

Unusual German 'Royal Trick' elephant tinplate mechanical money bank, 6in. long.

A 20th century English cold painted cast iron 'Stumps Speaker' money box, 10in. high.

Late 19th century American cast-iron mechanical bank, 'Paddy and the Pig', 8in. high.

Cast iron 'Novelty Bank' money box with hinged front, 6½in. high, American, circa 1875.

Late 19th century American Uncle Sam cast-iron mechanical bank by Shepard Hardware Co., 11½in. high.

Late 19th century American cat and mouse money box, 8½in. high.

A late 19th century American cold painted cast iron money box in the form of a soldier who fires a penny into a tree stump.

Late 19th century cast-iron 'Swiss Chalet' money box, 7in. high.

20th century English cast iron Artillery bank in the form of a cannon which fires coins into a pill box.

Swiss cylinder music box with drum, bells and butterflies, 27¼in. wide, in rosewood case.

Small carved music box showing three bears, 9in. high.

English 'Puck' phonograph, circa 1905.

Academy gramophone with bell-shaped tinplate horn, circa 1930, 13in. square.

His Master's Voice 510, with pleated diaphragm, 1924-25.

Edison Home phonograph with Bettini attachment.

Early 20th century German symphonium disc musical box, 10½in. wide.

Interesting Robeyphone gramophone, English, 1915-25, 10in. turntable.

Late 19th century walnut cased polyphon made for H. Peters & Co., London.

Swiss flute basse, voix celeste, interchangeable cylinder musical box by Langdorff et Fils, circa 1850.

Operaphone gramophone, circa 1925-30, 3ft. high.

Early 20th century symphonium disc musical box, 1ft. wide, German.

Good Edison Amberola VIII phonograph, American, circa 1913.

Regina music and gum machine in oak case with glass door, 16in. wide.

Early 20th century Swiss Britannia disc musical box, 1ft.9½in. high.

Mini record player with case, circa 1910, 8in. high.

Tanzbar accordion roller organ in black case, closed width 11in. wide.

Symphonium by C. Wheatstone, London, circa 1830, 2¾in. high.

Small cornet by Boosey & Co., London, circa 1880, 7½in. long.

French hurdy-gurdy by Jean-Baptiste Pajot, 1795, 26¼in. long.

Late 18th century English guitar by John Preston, London, 14in. long.

Late 19th century Faience model horn decorated in green, orange and blue on a white ground, probably French.

Unlabeled violin with two-piece back 14¼in. long, circa 1860, in shaped leather case.

Mid 19th century Ophicleide, 41in. long.

French pedal harp by Cousineau, Paris, circa 1775, 5ft. 3¾in. high.

Unusual trumpet by Kohler, London, 24in. long, circa 1865.

Attractive Dital harp by Edward Light, London, the simulated rosewood body in seven sections, circa 1815, 34½in. high.

English serpent by D'Almaine & Co., London, early 19th century, length 7ft. 7in.

Edinburgh made set of bagpipes with the Gordon tartan.

Late 17th century Italian virginals in a leather bound case.

Late 17th century Cor de Chasse, 165½in. long.

Neapolitan mandoline by Antonio Vinaccia, 1763, 22½in. long.

NETSUKE

Wood netsuke of a baby boy, signed Shumin saku.

Mid 19th century ivory netsuke, signed Mitsusada.

Unsigned 19th century wood netsuke.

Japanese ivory netsuke of a puppy pulling a string, signed.

Superb horse and foal netsuke by Rantei.

Wood and ivory netsuke of a young boy holding some fruit, signed on red lacquer Hideyuki.

Early 19th century Kyoto School netsuke of a Kirin.

Ivory netsuke of a monkey with young, signed Sadayoshi.

19th century ivory netsuke of a rat-catcher, signed Hansaku.

Large ivory netsuke study of a wolf with human skull, signed Tomonobu.

Small wood netsuke of Shoki seated on a sack, signed Ryukei.

Ivory netsuke of Longarms, 3in. high.

Ivory mask netsuke.

19th century trick netsuke by Tomomasa.

Netsuke of Tamamo No Mae and the Fox with Nine Tails, 2in. high.

Carved ivory netsuke of a monkey in a shell.

One of a pair of William and Mary capstan salts, 2¼in. high, circa 1690.

Liberty & Co. 'Tudric' pewter and enamel biscuit box and cover, 14cm. high, after 1903.

Fine late William and Mary posset pot in pewter, 9½in. wide, circa 1695.

Liberty & Co. pewter muffin dish and cover by Archibald Knox, circa 1905, 29cm. wide.

Large Maurel Art Nouveau patinated metal jardiniere, circa 1900, 29cm. high.

Pewter cornucopia chariot with Cupid, circa 1880, 10in. high.

Large WMF pewter jardiniere, 32.5cm. wide, circa 1900.

Urania pewter bucket and cover with fixed arched handle, stamped, 28.5cm. high, circa 1900.

Late 18th century German flask, 8¾in. high, in pewter.

WMF pewter candlestick, 26.25cm. high, circa 1900.

Early Georgian pewter tankard by Richard Going, 6½in. high, circa 1725.

WMF green glass and pewter claret jug of trumpet form, 40.5cm. high.

A fine wavy-edged plate by Thomas Chamberlain, 9½in. diam., circa 1760.

Rare, William & Mary pewter candlestick, 6½in. high, circa 1690.

Queen Anne plate with gadrooned border by John Shorey, 9in. diam., circa 1710.

Rare mid 17th century Saxon spouted flagon in pewter, with double-domed cover, 33cm. high.

A rare trencher salt of bulbous type with incised reeding around waist, 1¾in. high, circa 1700.

Charles II porringer of booged type, 7.1/8in. diameter, circa 1680.

18th century pewter barber's bowl of oval outline, 11¾in. wide.

Small, pewter Continental lidded tankard.

Fine, small, Charles II 'wriggled work' tankard by L.A., 6in. high, circa 1680.

Liberty & Co. 'Tudric' pewter stand with glass liner, circa 1905, 16.5cm. high.

'Diamond-point' pewter spoon with stem and terminal of pentagonal section, 6½in. long.

An attractive strawberry dish, the booge fluted into eighteen petal-shaped panels, 5in. diam., circa 1720.

Polished pewter water jug with cane handle by Liberty & Co., circa 1905.

A Bernese Stegkanne by Daniel Hemman from the first half of the 18th century, 31.5cm. high.

Charles I pewter flagon with plain 'muffin' cover, circa 1630-40, 11½in. high.

Silvered metal plaque 'The Spirit of Christmas', by John G. Hardy, circa 1895, 41cm. long.

18th century Swiss pewter covered Glockencanne with fixed ring carrying handle, 12in. high.

Set of seven waved-edged pewter dishes, 9½in. across, by George Beeston.

One of a pair of painted pewter mantel ornaments, circa 1790, 12¼in. high.

Deep-welled 'Mount Edgecumbe' bowl with broad rim, 14in. diam., circa 1640.

Porringer with finely pierced and shaped ear by Adam Banckes of Chester, 7½in. diam., circa 1700.

German silvered metal box, circa 1905, 16cm. wide.

Large metal tazza, 44cm. high, WMF marks, 1900-1910.

Art Nouveau pewter framed mirror from a model by Charles Jonchery, 72cm. wide.

15th century pewter spoon with latten 'scepter' knop, possibly unique, 5¾in. long.

Liberty & Co. 'Tudric' pewter tea and coffee service, circa 1910.

Rare lidless pewter tavern pot, by IG, 5in. high, circa 1720-30.

One of a pair of WMF silvered pewter and brass two-branch candelabra, 25cm. high.

19th century South German hexagonal pewter cannister, 13in. high.

Early 18th century pewter wrigglework plate with single reeded border, 8½in. diam.

Pewter spouted flagon of spreading cylindrical shape, 15¼in. high, spout with hinged cover.

Rare Saxon pewter tankard, probably by Hans Wildt the younger, 6¼in. high, circa 1590-1600.

18th century German Peterskirchen stoneware handled jug with pewter lid, 18in. high.

18th century Swiss pewter covered flagon with domed hinged cover, 12½in. high.

German or Bohemian pewter passover plate, circa 1803, 34.3cm. diam.

Bud baluster measure of half pint capacity, by John Carr, touch dated 1697, 5¼in. tall.

WMF pewter mounted green glass decanter, circa 1900, 42cm. high.

18th century German pewter Wasserbehalter by Georg **Ludwig Ruepprecht, Memmingen, 12½in. high.**

William and Mary pewter candlestick, 6in. high, circa 1690-96.

Mid 18th century Bernese Stegkanne with hexagonal spout, 34.5cm. high.

Bavarian pewter dish, rim embossed with flower petals, circa 1800, 41.7cm. diam.

19th century European pewter communion flagon with double domed hinged lid, 14in. high.

Liberty & Co. 'Tudric' pewter tea service by Archibald Knox.

Late 16th century 'horse-hoof' knop spoon, 6½in. long.

18th century German pewter mounted stoneware flagon with applied white decoration, 13½in. high.

Kayserzinn pewter jug, circa 1905, 26.75cm. high.

Gilbert Parks pewter charger, 20¼in. diam., dated 1899.

Edelzinn pewter jug, circa 1901, 33.5cm. high.

A Queen Anne tankard by Adam Banks of Milngate, the drum encircled by a single fillet at waist, 17.5cm high, circa 1710.

Dutch wriggleworked Corporation dish in pewter, circa 1661.

Dutch pewter beaker, Amsterdam, circa 1760.

Commonwealth pewter tankard, circa 1650, 5¾in. high.

Upright oak Broadwood 'Manxman' piano, circa 1900, 56½in. wide.

Square piano by John Broadwood, London, 1795, 5ft.2½in. long.

Upright iron framed piano by John Brinsmead, London.

Eavestaff 'minipiano pianette' with matching stool, 86cm. wide, 1930's.

Steinway grand piano with full marquetry inlays.

17th century Italian octavino in cypress case, on oak Regency style stand.

20th century red lacquer chinoiserie baby grand piano by Bluthner.

Important spinet by James Scoular, London circa 1765, length of back 73in.

Mid 19th century Viennese 'giraffe' piano, 7ft. 7in. high, in rosewood case.

English grand pianoforte by John Broadwood & Son, London 1804, 7ft. 5½in. long.

Sycamore cased baby grand by Strohmenger.

Early 19th century neoclassic German walnut piano by Michael Rosenberger, 79in. high.

Early 20th century Bechstein piano in mahogany case.

French combined piano and toilet table, circa 1820, 28in. wide.

Strohmenger painted satinwood baby grand piano and duet stool.

Street barrel piano, circa 1900, 3ft.4in. wide.

Late 19th/early 20th century Austrian Meerschaum cheroot holder, 17cm. long.

Large Meerschaum pipe with amber mouthpiece and heavily carved bowl, early 20th century, 28.5cm. long.

Well carved Meerschaum cigar holder in the form of a head of a Kaiser, 3¼in.

One of two late 19th century German Meerschaum pipes, 9½in. long.

Early 19th century block Meerschaum pipe with silver mounts, bowl 9½in. long.

Mid 19th century three-color glass pipe with knopped stem, 48.2cm. long.

Late 19th century Austrian Meerschaum pipe carved as the head of a negro boy, 17cm. long.

Meerschaum pipe with bowl supported by carved claw.

Austrian Meerschaum pipe, bowl carved as a young woman carrying a parasol, 20.3cm. long, circa 1880.

Erotic Meerschaum pipe holder, about 1885, 10½in. long.

Large Viennese Meerschaum bowl with silver mount, circa 1870, 20.3cm. long, in case.

Carved Meerchaum in the form of a dog and a snake in combat, 6in. long.

Meerschaum pipe, bowl carved as woman with a fur collar, circa 1900, 15.5cm. long, probably Austrian.

Late 19th century Austrian Meerschaum pipe, bowl carved as a hatching egg, 14.5cm. long.

Austrian Meerschaum pipe with carved bowl, circa 1905, 16.4cm. long, with case.

Mid 19th century American quilted patchwork coverlet, 72 x 90in.

Patchwork quilt with central flower medallion, circa 1820, 108in. square.

American patriotic coverlet in cotton sewn to give the effect of the American flag, 7ft.6in. square, circa 1880.

Civil War patriotic quilt, 68 x 88in., dated 1864.

Late 19th century bedcover made from officer's uniforms, 91½ x 77in.

Late 19th century American Victorian crazy quilt with matching shams, 76in. square.

Early 19th century patchwork quilt in hexagons, square and triangles, 94 x 87in.

19th century American pieced appliqued quilt with white cotton field, 102 x 82in.

Late 19th century embroidered bedspread on a midnight-blue satin ground, 99 x 85in.

Late 19th/early 20th century American patchwork quilt in navy blue and white triangles, 75½in. square.

18th century Portuguese coverlet, couchwork on Chinese silk, 100 x 80in.

19th century American appliqued and patchwork quilt, 88 x 94in.

Chintz patchwork bedcover with square central medallion and broad border, 65 x 60in.

Silk patchwork bedcover lined with Paisley pattern cotton, circa 1830. 89in. square.

Mid 18th century English 'Italian quilted' bedcover in white cotton, 103 x 93½in.

Pennsylvania pieced quilt of 'Spider's Web' pattern in multi-colored cottons, 84in. square, 1860-70.

Herat Beluchistan rug, circa 1900, 5ft. 11in. x 4ft. 3in.

Qashqai horse cover, 5ft. 4in. x 4ft. 1in., circa 1900.

Beluchistan Bakhtari prayer rug, circa 1900, 4ft. x 3ft.

Caucasian/Sileh rug with four rows of four 'Z' motifs, 3ft. 4in. x 8ft.7in.

Very fine silk Qum rug, 7ft. x 4ft. 8in.

A Yomut Ozmulduk, 2ft. 5in. x 4ft., circa 1850.

Pictorial Kirman rug, circa 1920, 2ft. 10in. x 2ft.

Orduj rug with triple medallion, circa 1880, 4ft.5in. x 3ft., in fair condition.

Dyrnak Yomut rug, 10ft. 7in. x 6ft. 8in., circa 1900.

Beluchistan rug in good condition, 4ft. 5in. x 3ft. 5in., circa 1880.

Armenian Kelim rug, circa 1880, 8ft. 10in. x 5ft. 2in.

Kuba rug, field of gray-blue with five medallions, dated 1347.

Mid 19th century South Persian antique Quash-gai bag, 0.61 x 0.61 m.

Kashan pictorial rug, 2ft.7in. x 1ft. 11in.

Attractive Templeton's carpet, by Charles Rennie Mackintosh, circa 1910, 455cm. x 358cm.

Fine Tabriz rug, field with indigo and ivory pole medallion, circa 1900, 5ft.7in. x 4ft.1in.

Early 19th century needlework sampler by Selina Doughty, 1835, framed and glazed, 38 x 32cm.

Fine spot-motif sampler on ivory linen ground, 20 x 6½in., circa 1630. framed.

William IV linen worked sampler by Fanney Wood, April, 1831, 17½in. square.

18th century needlework sampler by Mary Adamson, 1781, 31cm. high.

'Stone' family register by Anna Stone, 1810, 21½ x 15½in.

Needlework family record by Martha A. Chamberlain, Westmoreland, New Hampshire, 1833, 17 x 21in.

Unusual circular map sampler, 1804.

Embroidered border band sampler by Elizabeth Woodworth, 1758, 17¾ x 8½in.

Spot-motif sampler with geometric panels outlined with silver thread, circa 1630, framed, 20 x 8in.

Needlework sampler in circular reserve on linen ground, 1817, 20½ x 19½in.

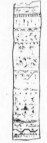

Early 17th century needlework sampler worked in cross stitch and running stitch, 86 x 16.5cm.

Mid 19th century needlework sampler by Ann Rebecca Willingham, 1842, 63 x 56cm.

Sampler worked with a house and a verse by Maria Norman, 1832, 16 x 12in.

Sampler by Elizabeth Brook, 1813, 15 x 11½in.

Needlework sampler by Sally Oliver, 1801, of Upper Beverley, America, 19½ x 21in.

Late 18th century needlework sampler, altered, framed and glazed, 31.5cm. square.

Early 18th century gold combined watch key and seal.

Victorian gold and bloodstone swivel seal.

Rare Chelsea seal, 7¼in. high, about 1758, possibly 'Girl in a Swing' style.

Victorian pinch-beck fob seal.

Fine silver and rock crystal swivel seal, 1½in. high, Dutch, circa 1740.

Gold mounted mother-of-pearl seal, circa 1825, 3¾in. high.

Early 19th century two-color musical fob seal, 1½in. high.

German steel swivel seal, early 18th century, 3¾in. high.

Mid 19th century Italian gold and hardstone desk seal, 8.3cm. high.

Rare English medieval jet seal, 2in. diam., 11th/12th century.

Silver hand seal and sealing wax holder.

Ivory seal carved with a squirrel on a grapevine, circa 1900, 7.5cm. high.

Faberge gold mounted desk seal with triple head.

A gold musical seal, circa 1820, 28mm. high.

Late 18th/early 19th century Italian lavastone desk seal with gold eyes, 11.5cm. high.

French gold mounted rock crystal desk seal, 5.4cm. high, circa 1910.

Shibayama and lacquer tsuba, signed, 4½in. high.

Japanese Shibayama and silver filigree tray, circa 1900, 30cm. wide.

19th century Japanese Shibayama and ivory brush pot, 5in. high.

Tomonobu Shibayama letter tray inlaid with mother-of-pearl and ivory, Japanese, circa 1900.

Elaborate Shibayama vase and cover, mother-of-pearl flower-heads, 6in. high, late 19th century.

One of a pair of Japanese Masayasu Shibayama vases, circa 1900.

19th century Japanese Shibayama display cabinet.

Japanese carved Shibayama and ivory figure, circa 1900, 15.5cm. high.

One of a pair of Minko enameled silver shibayama vases, circa 1900, 17.5cm. high, on wood stands.

Shibayama two-fold table screen, each leaf divided into two panels, 10½in. high.

Shibayama and ivory basket and cover with loop handle, circa 1900, 20cm. high.

Fine quality Japanese Shibayama incense burner.

Late 19th century Masahura shibayama elephant, inlaid with colored stones, 5cm. high.

One of a pair of gold and Shibayama vases, signed Yaschika, 12½in. high.

Finely carved Oriental ivory elephant decorated in Shibayama style, 28cm. high.

Masayasu shibayama ivory tusk vase, circa 1900.

Sunlight Soap, enamel sign of boy holding bars of Sunlight soap, 33½ x 32½in., circa 1905.

American kettle advertising sign in metal with iron handle, 22½in. high.

19th century Victorian butcher's shop sign of a carved bull's head, 13in. high, made of oak.

Copper fire insurance wall plaque 'Sun Fire Office 1710', mounted on oak panel.

Hodges Inn sign with oval shield, Vermont, circa 1790, 31¾in. wide.

'Selo Film' enamel sign in yellow, red and black, 14in. wide.

Double sided tavern sign 'The Bell', 40in. by 31in.

An English three-dimensional cardboard display, 4ft. high, circa 1920.

A rare English enameled advertising sign designed by the 'Beggarstaffs', 21in. x 14in., circa 1900.

A Barringer, Wallis & Manners Ltd. printed sign, 14in. high, circa 1910.

Morse's Distemper, enamel sign by Hassall, 60 x 40in.

Late 19th century carved wood tobacco sign, 3ft.8in. high.

Rare incised gray slate Bass Ale advertisement, circa 1890, 30in. high.

Courage counter model of a cockerel on a plinth, 1ft. high, circa 1931.

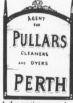

A decorative enamel sign, for 'Pullars of Perth', Cleaners and Dyers, 24in. high, circa 1920.

Trumans enameled pub sign 'The Flying Eagle', circa 1945, 3ft.6in. high.

BASKETS
CAKE

A fine pierced silver cake basket by Paul de Lamerie. 1731.

George III silver cake basket by Wm. Tuite, London, 1773, 14in., 19½oz.

George III oval shaped cake basket, 14¾in. wide, by Chawner & Emes, London, 1796, 21oz.11dwt.

Regency oblong cake basket by Benjamin and James Smith, 1810, 47oz., 13¼in. long.

SUGAR

Silver sugar basket by Peter and Anne Bateman, 4½oz.

Small George III pierced silver basket by Robt. Hennell, 1787, 4oz.

Small George III basket by Hester Bateman, London, 1789, 3in. wide.

Early 19th century German oval sugar vase on foot, 7oz.10dwt.

SWEETMEAT

George III silver gilt metal oval sweetmeat basket, 6¾in. wide, by Vere & Lutwyche, London, 1767, 6oz.5dwt.

George III boat-shaped sweetmeat basket, 6in. wide, by Henry Chawner, London, 1791, 8oz.3dwt.

George III octagonal silver footed sweetmeat basket, London, 1794, by Robt. Hennell.

George III boat-shaped silver sweetmeat basket, by Peter, Anne and William Bateman.

BEAKERS

One of a matching pair of silver gilt beakers by E. Barnard & Sons, London, 1862-68, 12.2cm. high, 748gm.

Early 18th century German silver gilt beaker by Esajas Busch, Augsburg, 1705, 3¼in. high, 4oz.12dwt.

Silver gilt and niello beaker, by E. C., Moscow, 1846, 6.7cm. high.

17th century German silver gilt beaker, 2⅛in. high, 2oz.18dwt.

BELLS

18th century Dutch table bell, 4¾in. high, by Jan Bot, Amsterdam, 1748, 8oz.18dwt.

Table bell by Elkington & Co. Ltd., Birmingham, 1890, 11.5cm. high.

George IV coronation bell, 5in. high, by T. Phipps & E. Robinson, London, 1820, 6oz. 19dwt.

Good Dutch silver gilt bell by Cornelis de Haan, The Hague, 1775, 5½in. high, 10oz.10dwt.

BISCUIT CONTAINERS

Circular biscuit barrel, 5½in. high, London, 1931, 17oz.6dwt.

Art Nouveau lantern style biscuitiere with glass liner, 1900.

E.P.N.S. oak biscuit barrel with ceramic lining, circa 1910.

George III circular biscuit barrel, 6¾in. high, by Solomon Hougham, London, 1801, 7oz.14dwt.

BOWLS

Late 17th century Dutch brandy bowl, by Thos. Sibrand Hicht, Dokkum, 1684, 8½in. wide, 5oz. 14dwt.

One of a pair of ornate Victorian silver bowls, 7in. diameter, London, 1899, 23oz.

Chinese export silver bowl, circa 1880.

George III Scottish circular bowl, by R. Gray & Son, Edinburgh, 1811, 8oz.8dwt., 5in. diam.

Jensen silver bowl and spoon, 10cm. high, circa 1947.

18th century Dutch tub-shaped covered bowl, 3½in. diam., by Marcelis de Haan, The Hague, 6oz. 5dwt.

Early Charles II bleeding bowl, 5½in. diam., London, 1664, 7oz.6dwt.

18th century silver gilt circular bowl and stand, 63oz.3dwt.

MONTEITH

William III Monteith bowl, by Robert Timbrell, London, 1698, 57oz.4dwt., 11in. diam.

Large sterling silver Monteith bowl with repousse decoration, with gilded lining, by Charles Harris, London, 1876.

William III Monteith bowl, by Robert Peake, London, 1700, 50oz. 10dwt., 11in. diam.

Large, late 18th century plated Sheffield Monteith bowl, 12in. high.

PUNCH

Silver punch bowl by William Davie, Edinburgh, 1785, 64oz.

Victorian punch bowl.

Rare early American silver punch bowl, by John Coney.

Large Victorian punch bowl, Birmingham, 1890, 14in. diameter.

ROSE

Victorian silver rosebowl, London, 1895, by Child & Child.

Mappin & Webb Ltd., circular three-handled rosebowl, London, 1918, 30.4cm. diam.

Indian silver rosebowl on stand.

Circular silver rosebowl, by Omar Ramsden, 1935, 70oz.18dwt., 11¾in. wide.

SUGAR

Early 19th century Russian sugar bowl, 6½in. wide, 1805, 17oz.17dwt.

Squat silver sugar bowl, by Abraham Pootholt and Jan van Giffen, 1779, 4in. high.

Liberty & Co. silver sugar basin and tongs, Birmingham, circa 1903-06, 4cm. high.

George II covered sugar bowl, 4½in. high, by Francis Crump, London, 1750, 9oz.18dwt.

BRANDY SAUCEPANS

Large George IV brandy saucepan and cover by James Scott, Dublin, 1824, 5½in. high, 21oz. 10dwt.

George III silver saucepan, 4in. high, by F. Knopfell, London, 1768, 19oz.9dwt.

Early George III brandy saucepan, 4½in. high, by Benjamin Brewood II, London, 1766, 19oz.1dwt.

George I brandy saucepan, 2¼in. high, by William Fleming, London, 1720, 5oz.17dwt.

BUCKLES

Silver belt buckle, 1892, 3¼in. long.

A Liberty silver and enamel buckle in the manner of Jessie M. King, Birmingham, 1908.

Rectangular Art Nouveau silver buckle, London, 1902, 5.5cm. wide.

Art Nouveau belt buckle, 7.75cm. wide, probably American, circa 1900.

CANDELABRA

One of a pair of Sheffield plated three-light candelabra.

Stylish German six-light candelabrum, circa 1910, 57cm. high, in silver colored metal.

One of two Victorian seven-light candelabra, 31½in. high, by Messrs. Barnard, 369oz.

One of a pair of Goldsmiths & Silversmiths Co., silver four-light candelabra, in 18th century style, 1902, 40.5cm. high.

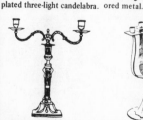

One of a pair of George III candelabra, 15¾in. high, by John Winter & Co., Sheffield, 1773.

Electroplated four-light candelabrum, stamped C. Kay, 1930's, 55cm. high.

One of a pair of 18th century German two-light candelabra, circa 1785, 56oz.2dwt., 14in. high.

One of a pair of silver gilt two-light candelabra, by J. Scofield, 1783, 16½in. high

CANDLESTICKS

One of a pair of William and Mary candlesticks, by F.S.S., London, 1690, 4½in. high, 16oz.8dwt.

One of a pair of silver candlesticks, London, 1894.

One of a pair of Martin Hall & Co. Ltd. table candlesticks, 23.5cm. high, London, 1893.

One of a pair of Edward Barnard & Sons table candlesticks, in the manner of Rundell, Bridge & Rundell, 1918, 2,360gm.

One of a pair of Wm. Hutton & Sons Ltd. table candlesticks, 28.5cm. high, London, 1910.

One of a set of four George III table candlesticks, by T. & J. Settle, Sheffield, 1815, 13½in. high.

One of four George II table candlesticks, by Paul de Lamerie, 6½in. high, London, 1731, 65oz.15dwt.

One of a pair of Dutch silver table candlesticks, Delft, 1677, 8½in. high, 29oz.

One of a set of four George II table candlesticks, by J. Cafe, 1750-52, 226oz., 10½in. high.

One of a pair of James Dixon & Sons large silver candlesticks, Sheffield, 1918, 30.5cm. high.

CARD CASES

Edwardian engine turned silver card case, Birmingham, 1905, 4in. tall.

Victorian tortoiseshell card case with silver string inlay, 4in. tall.

Austrian silver and enamel rectangular cigarette and card case, stamped.

Victorian parcel gilt woman's visiting card case by Edward Smith, Birmingham, 1850.

CASKETS

German silver rectangular casket, late 19th/early 20th century, 26.6cm. long, 1,116gm.

17th century Dutch marriage casket, 3in. wide, circa 1630, 3oz.17dwt.

George IV oblong commemorative casket, 8¾in. wide, by Joseph Angell, London, 1823, 29oz.14dwt.

An electroplated electrotype jewel casket, 10½in. long, by Alexandre Tahan, circa 1854.

CASTERS

George I octagonal caster, by Glover Johnson, London, 1717. 6oz.13dwt.

Queen Anne caster, London, 1713, by Charles Adams, 6½in. high, 7oz.

Queen Anne cylindrical caster with pierced lid, 6½in. high, 6oz.17dwt.

Silver sugar caster, 7in. high, London, 1934, 7oz. 5dwt.

CENTERPIECES

Large electroplated dessert stand with ivory stem, 1890's, 55.4cm.

Victorian centerpiece by Stephen Smith, 1874, 172oz., 15¼in. high.

WMF Art Nouveau German silver centerpiece, 1925, 30in. high.

Large Jensen silver coupe, London, 1922, 19.75cm. high.

CHALICES

18th century Italian chalice, by Giovanni Valadier, Rome, 10¼in. high, circa 1775, 24oz. 10dwt.

Rare German gilt metal chalice, by Marcus Purman, 1608, 12.4cm. high.

Elizabeth I chalice and cover, 1570, 7in. high, 8oz. 16dwt.

Rare Elizabethan Provincial chalice, 5¾in. high, Norwich, 1567, 6oz.18dwt.

CHAMBERSTICKS

Victorian taperstick, 4¼in. diam., by Charles Fox, 1838, 4oz.11dwt.

George II chamber candlestick, by Elizabeth Godfrey, London, 1750, 6in. high, 14oz.

George III chamber candlestick by R. & S. Hennell, London, 1802, 10oz., 5¼in. diameter.

James II chamber candlestick, 3½in. diam., 2oz., maker's mark T.E.

CHOCOLATE POTS

Rare George III baluster chocolate pot, by R. Williams, Dublin, circa 1770, 10in. high, 36oz.

Queen Anne tapered cylindrical chocolate pot, by R. Timbrell and J. Bell, London, 1711, 25oz.11dwt., 10in. high.

18th century German chocolate pot, 7¼in. high, by Johann Heinrich Menzel, Augsburg, circa 1735, 15oz.1dwt.

Short spouted chocolate pot, by David Willaume, Jnr., 1744, 10¼in. high, 45oz.10dwt., with wickerwork handle.

CIGARETTE CASES

Silver and enamel cigarette case, 1925, 8.4cm. high.

Russian silver cigarette case enameled in dark blue orange, green and claret.

German enameled cigarette case on silver colored metal, circa 1910, 9.4cm. high.

Silver Art Nouveau cigarette case, Birmingham, 1905, 9cm. high.

CLARET JUGS

John Foligno claret jug, London, 1806.

Cut glass and silver claret jug, complete with stopper, 1902.

Saunders & Shepherd silver mounted glass claret jug, London, 1895, 20.4cm. high.

Late 19th century silver mounted cut glass claret jug.

COASTERS

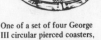

One of a pair of William IV wine coasters, 5¾in. diam.

One of four Russian shaped circular wine coasters by Nichols & Plinke, 1859.

One of a set of four George III circular pierced coasters, by R. Hennell, 12.5cm. diam.

One of a pair of George IV wine coasters by J. Crouch and W. Reid, London, 1821, 6¼in. diam.

COFFEE POTS

Silver coffee pot by S. Hennell, London, 1841, 34oz.

Silver gilt coffee pot, 1823, on a heater stand, 8in. high, by Wm. Eley.

Fine cylindrical silver chocolate pot, 1725, 9in. high, 26oz.10dwt., made by Joseph Clare.

A magnificent George II silver coffee pot, by de Lamerie, made in 1738.

18th century Swiss coffee pot, 8¼in. high, Geneva, circa 1770, 16oz.

George III baluster coffee pot, by Benjamin Gignac, London, 1767, 11¼in. high, 31oz.15dwt.

Side-handled coffee pot, by David Tanqueray, 9½in. high, 33oz.10dwt.

Vase-shaped silver coffee pot, by Daniel Smith and Robert Sharp, 1776, 11in. high, 24oz.

CREAM BOATS

George II Scottish cream boat, by John Main, Edinburgh, 1739, 6½in. wide, 7oz.14dwt.

Irish George III silver cream boat, Dublin 1811.

George II cream boat 5¼in., by William Cripps, London, 1743, 6oz.2dwt.

George III silver cream boat, by Wm. Harrison, 1763.

CRUETS

George III oblong silver gilt egg cruet by John Emes, London, 1806, 37oz.6dwt., 7¼in. wide.

Jensen silver cruet, circa 1950-55.

George III cruet frame, by Paul Storr, 11½in. high, 31oz.1dwt., with six cut glass bottles.

George III oval cruet frame and bottles, by Robert and David Hennell, London, 1799.

CUPS

Edwardian silver double-handled prize cup, 5oz. 5dwt.

Coconut cup with 17th century silver mounts, bearing an inscription, 3½in. diam.

Silver loving cup, by Hester Bateman, circa 1789.

Commonwealth two-handled cup and cover, marked on base and lid, maker's mark A. F. in a shaped shield, London, 1653.

George II silver gilt two-handled cup and cover, by John Le Sage, London, 1736, 24oz.1dwt., 8¼in. high.

Standing cup, by Omar Ramsden, 7¼in. high, London, 1938, 24oz. 15dwt.

Wm. Hutton & Sons Ltd., twin-handled silver cup, 28cm. high, London, 1902.

Charles S. Harris & Son Ltd., two-handled cup and cover, London, 1904, 30.7cm. high, 1,924gm.

CAUDLE

CHRISTENING

Commonwealth silver gilt caudle cup and cover, by N. Wollaston, London, 1656, 4½in. high, 13oz.12dwt.

Charles II caudle cup and cover, by Garthorne, London, 1682, 22oz.6dwt., 6½in. high.

18th century Channel Islands christening cup, 2¾in. high.

Silver Victorian christening cup, by J. Angel, 1851, 4oz.

STIRRUP

TUMBLER

Late 18th century fox mask stirrup cup.

One of a pair of George III parcel gilt stirrup cups, by John Carter, London, 1773.

18th century Norwegian parcel gilt tumbler cup, 1oz.9dwt., 1¾in. high.

One of a set of three early 18th century parcel gilt tumbler cups, circa 1700, 9oz.2dwt.

CUPS
WINE

James I silver gilt wine cup, 8in. high, London, 1610, 10oz.12dwt.

One of a pair of George III Scottish wine cups, 7in. high, Edinburgh, 1805, 22oz.16dwt.

George III wine cup, 6in. high, by Hester Bateman, London, 1787, 5oz. 19dwt.

Unusual Charles II wine cup, circa 1675, 3½in. high, 2oz.6dwt.

DISHES

Silver chafing dish with Belgian hall marks, 1772.

18th century East European parcel gilt dish and cover, 10¾in. diam. 22oz.5dwt.

Victorian Irish potato dish, Dublin, 1896, 10in. diam., 24oz.

Hukin & Heath silver sweetmeat dish, 14cm. high, London, 1881.

17th century Dutch silver embossed dish, maker's mark H.N., Hague, 1666, 82oz.

WMF silvered metal dish, circa 1900, 17.5cm. high.

One of a pair of George I silver gilt strawberry dishes, 8½in. diam., London, 1719, 24oz.18dwt.

Breakfast dish and cover in Sheffield Plate, about 1820.

ENTREE

One of a pair of Victorian, shaped oval entree dishes and covers by R. Garrard, 1848, 13½in. long, 120oz.

George III entree dish and cover, 12¼in. wide, by J. Edwards, London, 41oz. 14dwt.

One of a set of four George IV octagonal entree dishes and covers, 10¾in. wide, by Wm. Eley, London, 1827, 205oz.16dwt.

George III silver oblong entree dish and cover by Paul Storr, London, 1808, 63oz.5dwt.

DISHES
FRUIT

Boat-shaped silver openwork fruit dish by Mappin & Webb, Sheffield, 1913, 752gm.

George IV oval fruit dish, 30in. wide, by Marshall & Sons, Edinburgh, 151oz.

Italian two-handled shaped oval fruit dish, 20th century, 48cm. wide, 1,271gm.

MEAT

George III oval meat dish, 16in. wide, by William Burwash, London, 1817, 49oz.10dwt.

Kayserzinn meat dish and cover, 55cm. long, circa 1900.

One of a pair of George II oval meat dishes, by Simon Jouet, 1759, 18in. long, 124oz.

SWEETMEAT

A very fine silver sweetmeat box, maker's mark B.B. with a crescent below, London, 1676, 18.4cm., 21oz.12dwt.

Charles I circular shaped sweetmeat dish, 6¼in. diam., London, 1638, 4oz.16dwt.

17th century German sweetmeat dish, Augsburg, circa 1675, 5¼in. wide, 2oz.9dwt.

German oval sweetmeat dish, circa 1685, 2oz. 10dwt., 5in. wide.

VEGETABLE

One of a pair of George III circular vegetable dishes and covers, 9¼in. diam., by Wakelin & Garrard, London, 1796, 64oz.12dwt.

One of a pair of George III plain circular vegetable dishes and covers, 10½in. diam., by Paul Storr, 1808, 116oz.

One of a pair of Victorian silver vegetable dishes on warming stands.

George III circular vegetable dish and cover, by Paul Storr, London, 1796, 107oz. 1dwt., 12¾in. diam.

EPERGNES

Silver plated epergne, circa 1825, 15½in. high.

George III epergne, by Emick Romer, London, 1770, 91oz. 19dwt., 17¼in. high.

Silver epergne by A. H., London, 1864.

George III epergne, 15¼in. high, by Thos. Pitts, London, 1774, 129oz.12dwt.

EWERS

17th century Italian ewer, Naples, 24oz.10dwt., 9in. high.

Russian silver ewer and basin, St. Petersburg, 1841.

17th century helmet-shaped ewer, 7¼in. high, 21oz.4dwt.

American silver flask-shaped wine ewer and tray by Gorham Mfg. Co., Providence, R. I. 1882, 1,027gm.

FISH SERVERS

Silver fish trowel by Richard Williams, 1770, 13in. long.

Pair of late 19th century fish servers with bone handles, circa 1880.

18th century Dutch serving slice, 15¼in. long, by Wm. Pont, Amsterdam, 1772, 6oz.14dwt.

FLAGONS

George IV cylindrical flagon by R. Emes and E. Barnard, 1826, 61oz.

Victorian silver flagon, 11in. high, by John Mitchell, Glasgow, 1854, 39oz.16dwt.

Silver replica of a late 17th century flagon, by Lambert & Co., London, 1908, 1,563gm.

One of two late 17th century small flagons, 9in. high, 56oz.7dwt.

SILVER

FLATWARE

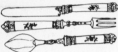
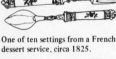

One of ten settings from a French dessert service, circa 1825.

Three pieces of silver, by Charles Rennie Mackintosh.

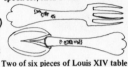

Dutch traveling knife, fork and **spoon set, circa 1700.**

Pair of plated salad servers made in 1920's.

Pair of 18th century oyster forks, Old English thread.

Two of six pieces of Louis XIV table silver by Louis Nicolle, circa 1687.

One of a set of twelve silver gilt spoons, made in 1592.

Rare early 17th century French two-prong fork.

Charles II silver spoon with rare boar's head finial.

George III silver caddy spoon by Samuel Pemberton, London 1807.

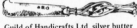

Guild of Handicrafts Ltd. silver butter knife, circa 1900, 13.5cm. long.

Tablespoon by Hester Bateman, London, 1766.

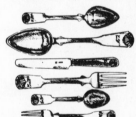

Part of a George III crested hour glass pattern set of table silver by Wallis & Hayne, London, 116oz.10dwt.

Part of a Reed & Barton extensive canteen of 'Francis I' pattern tableware, 301oz., circa 1949.

19th century German table silver by J.F. Brahmfeld, Hamburg, 117oz.

Part of forty-four pieces of table silver, by Omar Ramsden, London, 1926-38, 54oz.8dwt.

Fine Georg Jensen silver flatware service, circa 1910.

Part of a silver gilt dessert service, 1824-32, 118oz. 15dwt.

GOBLETS

One of a pair of silver gilt German goblets, 17th century.

Late 19th century Russian cup-shaped goblet, 4¼in. high, 5oz.9dwt.

HONEY POTS

Silver gilt honey pot and matched stand, by Paul Storr, 1798, 4¾in. high, 14oz.

George III 'Skep' honey pot and stand, London, 1798-1800, 12oz.17dwt., 4¾in. high.

INKSTANDS

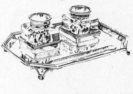

George II rectangular inkstand, 9¾in. wide, by William Shaw, London, 1730, 24oz.16dwt.

Two-bottle silver inkstand, by Burrage Davenport, London, 1777, 4in. long, 4oz.

Harrods Ltd., two-bottle inkstand on molded octagonal base, by R.W. Burbridge, London, 1936, 790gm.

Edwardian silver plated inkstand by Mappin and Webb, about 1910.

George III oblong inkstand, 8in. wide, by Susanna Barker, London, 1770, 20oz. 7dwt.

George III silver inkstand by Paul Storr, London 1803, 14¼in. wide.

JUGS

George III baluster silver jug with embossed decoration.

George IV small brandy jug on stand with burner, 7¾in. high, by J. Angell, London 1825, 16oz. 19dwt.

Silver jug, by Abraham Pootholt and Jan van Giffen, 6in. high, 1784.

Victorian 'Cellini' jug with hinged lid, 14½in. high, London 1884, 42oz.

JUGS
BEER

George II baluster beer jug, 8½in. high, by Thos. Coffin, Exeter, 1734, 28oz.7dwt.

George I covered beer jug, by John Edwards, London, 1719, 10in. high, 32oz. 19dwt.

George II plain pear-shaped beer jug by Wm. Grundy, 1750, 7¾in. high, 28oz.

George II baluster shaped silver beer jug, by Wm. Darker, London. 1730, 25oz.

COFFEE

18th century baluster shaped silver coffee jug, 7in. high, 11.9oz.

George III coffee jug on stand, 12in. high, by Paul Storr, London 1807, 54oz. 11dwt.

George III baluster coffee jug by Wm. Bruce, London, 1814, 21oz.19dwt., 8¾in. high.

Vase-shaped fluted coffee jug, by Ambrose Boxwell, Dublin, circa 1775, 27½oz.

CREAM

Georgian silver cream jug, 3½oz., circa 1820.

George III silver cow creamer, 5¾in. long, by John Schuppe, 1765, 5oz.12dwt.

George II circular cream jug, by Thos. Sutton, Dublin, 1735, 3¼in. high, 4oz.10dwt.

George III helmet-shaped cream jug, 5¾in. high, London, 1793, 3oz.13dwt.

MILK

George III helmet-shaped milk jug, by Robert Sharp, London, 1793, 5in. high, 7oz.8dwt.

George III milk jug, by Hester Bateman, London, 1777, 6½in. high, 6oz. 12dwt.

George III Scottish provincial covered milk jug, by John Baillie, Inverness, circa 1780, 4¾in. high, 8oz.4dwt.

George II Newcastle milk jug, 4½in. high, by Wm. Whitfield, 1742, 4oz. 19dwt.

JUGS
WATER

A fine Hester Bateman baluster hot water jug, 1783.

William IV silver water jug, London, 1837.

George III hot water jug, by Thos. Wynn, London, 1777, 26oz., 11in. high.

Late Georgian hot water jug, London, 1831, 27½oz., 10½in. high.

WINE

Queen Anne Irish wine jug, by Thos. Boulton of Dublin, 1702.

Silver wine jug by John S. Hunt, London, 1850, 13½in. high.

George II Irish, covered jug, by Erasmus Cope, Dublin, 1736, 33oz.8dwt.

George III baluster wine jug.

KOVSCH

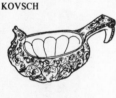

Superb silver Russian kovsch, probably by Maria Somenova.

Enameled silver gilt kovsch by Carl Faberge, circa 1913, 7in. long.

19th century Russian kovsch in silver and enamel inlaid with green and red stones.

Enameled silver kovsch by Carl Faberge, circa 1910, 2½in. long.

LADLES

One of a pair of George II Hanoverian pattern sauce ladles, by Elias Cachart, London, 1744, 5oz.5dwt.

Fluted silver punch ladle, by E. Aldridge, 1742.

Bright cut ladle, by R. Keay, Perth, 1790.

LEMON STRAINERS

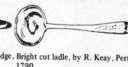

Silver lemon strainer, by H. Northcote, 1799.

George I silver lemon strainer, Francis Nelme, London, 1727.

Late 18th century, bright cut silver strainer, 10in. across.

MODELS

Late 19th century silver model of a bull, 72oz. 13dwt., 18¼in. overall.

One of a pair of Portuguese 19th century models of Kylins, 106oz., 14½in. high.

Crane with silver body and copper beak, circa 1900, 5¾in. high.

One of a pair of B. Neresheimer & Sohne figures of knights, Hanau, 1911, 2,795gm.

MUGS

George III silver christening mug, London, 1798, by John Emes, 3oz.

A small slightly tapering silver beer mug with scroll handle, London, 1801, 8½oz.

George III silver pint baluster mug, by John Deacon, 1769, 5in. high, 10½oz.

Charles II tapering cylindrical mug, by Jonah Kirk, London, 1683, 9oz. 8dwt., 4in. high.

MULLS

Silver mounted horn snuff mull, probably Tain, circa 1837.

Scottish horn mull with silver mounts, 8¾in. long, circa 1760.

Silver mounted ram's head table snuff mull, about 1880, 13½in. high.

Scottish snuff mull, circa 1800.

MUSTARDS

Italian mustard pot and stand, Naples, 1792, stand 4½in. diam., 7oz.10dwt.

Early Victorian mustard pot by Charles Fox, London, 1837, 3in. high, 4oz.12dwt.

Charles T. and George Fox owl shaped mustard pot, 11.5cm. high, 9.9oz.

George III barrel-shaped mustard pot, by Robert and David Hennell, London, 1798, 3in. high, 3oz.13dwt.

SILVER

NEFS

Continental two-masted nef on four wheels, circa 1900, 15¼in. high.

Late 19th century silver Dutch nef, 24in. long, mounted on a carriage.

Late 19th century German nef on dolphin stem, with pseudo hallmarks, 732gm.

Continental two-masted nef on four wheels, 17½in. high, dated for 1901.

NUTMEGS

Late 18th century egg-shaped nutmeg grater, by Samuel Meriton.

Silver nutmeg grater by Elkington & Co., Birmingham, 1906, 3in. long.

George III silver nutmeg grater, by Mary Hyde and John Reily, London, 1799, 2in. diam.

Georgian silver nutmeg grater, by Phipps & Robinson, London, 1788, 2¾in. high.

PAP BOATS

Georgian silver pap boat, maker's mark TE, 4¾in., 2oz.

Unmarked silver and coconut shell pap boat, circa 1760, 5in. long.

George III silver pap boat, by Rebecca Emes and Edward Barnard, 2½oz.

PEPPERS

George I cylindrical kitchen pepper, by John Hamilton, Dublin, 2½in. high, 2oz.9dwt.

Pair of silver mounted Victorian ivory pepper-ettes.

One of two Handicrafts Ltd. pepper casters, circa 1900, 6.5cm. high.

Gallia cruet set, 8cm. high, in silvered metal, 1920's.

PHOTOGRAPH FRAMES

Art Nouveau silver photograph frame, 6in. high.

Liberty & Co. silver and enamel frame, Birmingham, 1910, 27cm. high.

One of two Liberty & Co. silver frames, Birmingham, 1905, 19.25cm. high.

Silver Art Nouveau photograph frame by J. & A. Zimmerman, 29cm. high, Birmingham, 1903.

PLATES

One of twelve George III dinner plates by Paul Storr, London, 1807, 10½in. diam., 271oz.7dwt.

One of twelve George III shaped circular dinner plates, 9¾in. diam., by L. Herne and F. Butty, London, 1762, 212oz.15dwt.

George I Irish circular plate, 9in. diam., Dublin, 1725, 13oz.13dwt.

One of twelve George II dinner plates, 9¾in. diam., by G. Methuen, London, 1756, 196oz.6dwt.

PORRINGERS

Two-handled George V silver porringer, London, 1915.

Queen Anne porringer on collet foot, 1713, 6oz.

Charles II two-handled porringer, 4½in. high, 13oz. 13dwt.

Charles II plain two-handled porringer on rim foot, probably West Country, maker's mark IP, circa 1670, 6oz. 3dwt.

PURSES

Stylish German silver mesh evening purse, circa 1910, 18cm. long.

Art Nouveau silver purse, 1908.

La Minauderie, silver engine turned evening bag by C. van Cleef and Arpels, about 1935.

18th century Dutch silver gilt bag mount, maker's mark I.V.I., Amsterdam 1749, 3oz. 15dwt.

QUAICH

Queen Anne quaich, by Robt. Ker, Edinburgh, circa 1710.

A typical Stuart quaich, 7¾in. diam, unmarked, Scottish, circa 1675.

Large two-handled circular quaich, unmarked, circa 1680, 7in. diam., 10oz.

RATTLES

Victorian silver rattle dated 1886.

Early 18th century child's silver rattle, 5¼in. long, circa 1700.

17th century child's rattle bearing the Edinburgh date letter for 1681.

SALTS

One of a set of four George II capstan salts, London, 1754, by G. Wickes, 32oz.

One of a pair of George III silver salts of spool-shape, London, 1792, 6oz.

One of a pair of late 18th century silver gilt salts, complete with spoons, 23oz.

One of a pair of George III oval salt cellars by Paul Storr, London, 1812, 4½in. wide, 18oz.4dwt.

One of a set of four George III double salts, 4¼in. wide, by J. Scofield, London, 1784, 28oz.15dwt.

One of a pair of Queen Anne trencher salt cellars, by B. Bentley, 3in. diam., 4oz.2dwt.

One of a pair of silver salt cellars by Robert Garrard, 3¼in. high.

One of a set of four George III oval tub-shaped silver salts, London, 1808, 12½oz.

SALVERS

George II triangular salver by George Methuen, London, 1752, 16oz.4dwt., 9½in. wide.

Victorian Scottish shaped circular presentation salver, 18in. diam., Edinburgh, 1846, 70oz.18dwt.

George II plain shaped square silver salver, by Robert Abercrombie.

George III shaped circular salver, 11¼in. diam., by J. Carter, London, 1773, 24oz.2dwt.

SAUCEBOATS

One of a pair of Victorian sauceboats, 8¼in. long, by Robert Garrard, London, 1847, 41oz.19dwt.

George IV oval sauceboat by E. E. J. & W. Barnard, London, 1829, 7in. wide, 17oz.1dwt.

One of a pair of George II oval sauceboats, by Wm. Cripps, London, 1754, 8in. wide, 28oz.8dwt.

One of a pair of George III oval sauceboats, by Thos. Evans, London, 1775, 34oz. 7dwt., 7½in. wide.

SCISSORS

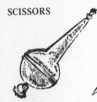   

Silver gilt mounted mother-of-pearl scissor case, circa 1700.

Ornate Victorian silver scissors and matching thimble, Birmingham 1890.

Gilt and silver metal scissors and paper knife, circa 1935.

Tang silver gilt scissors, 7½in. long.

SCOOPS

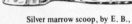  

Silver marrow scoop, by E. B., London, 1745.

Silver Stilton cheese scoop, 1931.

Combined silver marrow scoop and tablespoon, by Elias Cachart, 1750.

Stilton cheese scoop with ejector slide, Joseph Taylor, Birmingham, 1803.

Silver cheese scoop by Mary Chawner, 1840.

Rococo shell heel marrow spoon, George Smith, London, 1780.

SKEWERS

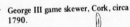

Silver skewer, maker's mark rubbed, London, 1779.

Pair of silver meat skewers, by Peter and Ann Bateman, 1798.

George III game skewer, Cork, circa 1790.

SNUFFERS

George III Irish boat-shaped tray and snuffers, by James Scott, Dublin, 8oz. 5dwt.

18th century Dutch silver snuffer stand and snuffers, by Jan Pondt of Bremen, Amsterdam, 1756, 9oz. 18dwt.

Charles II snuffer tray with matching snuffers, by W.B., 15oz.12dwt.

Queen Anne snuffers stand and a pair of snuffers, by Thos. Prichard, London, 1704, 11oz.17dwt.

SNUFF BOXES

Shaped rectangular silver snuff box with gilt interior by Ed. Smith, Birmingham, 1851, 7.2cm. long.

George III Irish silver snuff box, by A. Tuppy, Dublin, 1782, 3¼in. wide.

A rare late 18th century silver gilt 'mask' snuff box, 3in. wide.

William IV snuff box by Edward Shaw, Birmingham, 1834, 6oz.3dwt., 3¼in. wide.

TANKARDS

George II baluster shaped silver tankard, 1732.

Dutch silver mounted horn tankard with silver lining, with portrait of William and Mary on side.

Queen Anne cylindrical tankard, 8in. high, by Alice Sheene, London, 1709, 30oz. 8dwt.

Silver Augsburg tankard, circa 1700, 33oz., with embossed decoration.

Early George III tankard, 8in. high, by W.F., London, 1767, 15oz.1dwt.

Tankard given to Bismarck by Wilhelm I of Prussia, 24½in. high, 1871.

Swedish tankard of peg type, repousse decorated with figures and fruits.

George III tapering cylindrical tankard, by Peter and Anne Bateman, London, 1797, 7¼in. high, 26oz.6dwt.

TAPERSTICKS

George II taperstick, by J. Cafe, London, 1743, 4½in. high, 4oz.7dwt.

Silver taperstick, by E. Barnet, York, 1713, 2¾oz.

TAZZAS

18th century Dutch silver gilt tazza, by Casparus Janszonius Haarlem, 4¾in. diam., 3oz.14dwt.

WMF silvered metal tazza, 23.25cm. high, circa 1900.

TEA & COFFEE SETS

Victorian Scottish teaset by Marshall & Sons, Edinburgh, 1849, 40oz.8dwt.

Juventa Art Nouveau electroplated metal coffee service, circa 1900.

Three-piece coffee service by August Dufour, Belgium.

Late Victorian five-piece tea and coffee set by Smith, Sissons & Co., London, 61oz.

Three-piece tea service by Samuel Hennell, London, 1803, 28oz.

Four-piece silver tea service by John Angell, London, 1824.

TEA CADDIES

George III oval tea caddy, 5in. high, by Wm. Vincent, London, 1778, 3oz.10dwt.

George III oblong tea caddy, by P. Gillois, London, 1763, 11oz. 7dwt., 5½in. high.

One of a pair of George II tea caddies, 5¼in. high, by S. Taylor, London, 1756, 16oz.2dwt.

George IV tea caddy, by Charles Price, London, 1828, 18oz.4dwt., 6¼in. high.

George III silver tea caddy, by Rebecca Emes and Edward Barnard I, London, 1809, 22½oz.

Guild of Handicrafts Ltd. silver tea caddy, London, 1906, 7cm. high, on four ball feet.

Silver tea caddy by Paul de Lamerie, 1724, 13.3cm. high, 15oz.13dwt.

One of a pair of George I tea caddies, 5in. high, by G. Roode, London, 1715, 11oz.4dwt.

TEA KETTLES

Bruder Frank kettle and stand, circa 1900, in silver colored metal.

Victorian silver spirit kettle, by Robb & Whittet, Edinburgh, 1837, 74oz.

George II Irish tea kettle on lampstand, by John Taylor, 13in. high, 67oz.14dwt.

George I tea kettle on stand, 14in. high, by John White, London, circa 1720, 73oz. 9dwt.

TEAPOTS

George III oval teapot by Hester Bateman, 5in. high, London, 1784, 13oz.6dwt.

George III shaped oval teapot and stand, 7in. high, by Langlands & Robertson, Newcastle, 1791, 22oz.

Louis XVI cylindrical teapot, 4in. high, by Jacques Antoine Bonhomme, Paris, 1783, 12oz.11dwt.

Irish George IV silver teapot, Dublin, 1823, by Edward Power, 33oz.

Victorian plated teapot with ivory handle.

Swedish teapot, circa 1819, 21oz., 6in. high.

TOASTERS

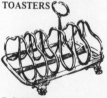   

Early Victorian six-section toast rack by Henry Wilkinson & Co., 1839, 8oz.

Victorian six-division silver toast rack, Birmingham, 1898, 9oz.5dwt.

Victorian toast rack by Robt. Garrard, London, 1869.

Heath & Middleton silver toast rack, 1899, 12.5cm. wide.

TOBACCO BOXES

18th century Dutch oblong tobacco box by Christoffel Woortman, Amsterdam, 1797, 6oz.6dwt., 6¼in. wide.

Queen Anne oval tobacco box, by Edward Cornock, London, 1709, 3¾in. wide, 3oz.16dwt.

17th century oval silver tobacco box, 4¼in. wide, circa 1680.

Dutch silver tobacco box, Leeuwarden, circa 1750, 22oz.10dwt.

TOILET REQUISITES

Queen Anne toilet service, London, circa 1706, 81oz.12dwt.

Portuguese silver and stained fish-skin necessaire de voyage, circa 1730-40.

Fine 19th century dressing case, London, 1838.

TONGS & NIPS

Silver rococo period nips enhanced with gilding, 1745.

Pair of Georgian silver asparagus servers.

George III bright cut sugar tongs, by G. Smith and T. Hayter, London, 1798.

Early 18th century silver sugar tongs, by L.E., London, circa 1710.

Pair of Scottish tongs by Hamilton & Inches, 1906, 48cm. fully extended.

Chased leaf tongs, by W. & J. Deane, London, circa 1765.

Silver asparagus tongs by G. W. Adams, 1864.

Pair of openwork silver tongs by Benjamin Montague, London 1760.

Silver asparagus tongs, by J. Buckett, of London, circa 1770, 23in. long.

TRAYS

George III two-handled tray, by J. Wakelin and R. Garrard, 1796, 80oz., 20in. long.

Large, heavy Walker & Hall two-handled rectangular tray, Sheffield, 1901, 75.2cm. wide, 5,086gm.

Embossed Indian silver tray, circa 1900, 21in. long.

Late 17th century Dutch spice tray, Rotterdam, circa 1683, 8½in. wide, 5oz.15dwt.

George II shaped triangular tea kettle stand on hoof feet, by R. Abercrombie, 1735, 14oz.11dwt.

Two-handled octagonal pierced gallery tea tray by Elkington & Co., London, 1913, 4,700gm.

TUREENS
SAUCE

One of a pair of George III oval sauce tureens and covers, 9¼in. wide, by D. Smith and R. Sharp, London, 1778, 47oz.7dwt.

One of a pair of George III sauce tureens by Wm. Bennett, London, 1808, 52oz.4dwt.

One of a pair of George III silver sauce tureens, by J. Carter, London, 1776, 45oz.

SOUP

Electroplated tureen and cover in the form of a broody hen, by G. R. Collins & Co., 1850's, 22cm. wide.

George II two-handled soup tureen and cover, Dublin 1745, 164oz., 13¾in. long.

George III oval soup tureen and cover, 15in. wide, by R. Garrard, London, 1814, 121oz.6dwt.

URNS

Early 18th century Scottish urn, 11½in. high, Edinburgh, circa 1725, 43oz.11dwt.

Vase-shaped tea urn, 16¼in. high, by Heath & Middleton, London, 1906, 78oz.4dwt.

George III tea urn, by C. Wright, London, 1771, 80oz.

Unusual George II pear-shaped chocolate urn.

VASES

George III sugar vase, by Robt. Hennell, London, 1784, 5in. high, 7oz.9dwt.

Large WMF electroplated electrotype vase, circa 1900, 49cm. high.

Jensen silver vase, London, 1930, 10.25cm. wide.

George III silver gilt covered vase, London, 1770, 20oz.6dwt., 8¼in. high.

VINAIGRETTES

Silver gilt oval vinaigrette by S. Pemberton, Birmingham, 1800.

Early Victorian silver gilt vinaigrette by N. Mills, London, 1838, 1½in. wide.

George IV silver gilt vinaigrette, 1½in. diam., by J. Willmore, Birmingham, 1824.

Silver vinaigrette by J. Butler, Birmingham, 1826.

WINE COOLERS

One of a pair of Catherine the Great wine coolers, by Z. Deichmann, 1766.

One of four George III two-handled campana-shaped wine coolers, 10in. high, 407oz.

One of a pair of George III wine coolers by Paul Storr, London, 1812, 9¾in. high, 242oz.

French vase-shaped wine cooler, 10in. high, circa 1890, 65oz.

WINE FUNNELS

George III wine funnel by George Fenwick, 1817.

George III funnel, by Thos. Graham, London, 1795, 4¼in. high, 1oz.4dwt.

Silver wine funnel by G. Lowe, 1824, 14cm. long.

Georgian silver wine funnel, London, 1811, by E. Morley.

WINE LABELS

George III wine label, engraved for claret, by M. Binley, London, circa 1770.

George IV pierced wine label 'Madeira', by Rawlings & Sumner, 1830.

Rare 18th century wine label apparently unmarked, circa 1780.

Victorian wine label, pierced 'Brandy' by Edward and John Barnard, London, 1853.

WINE TASTERS

William III wine taster, London 1695, 3oz.3dwt.

Mid 17th century wine taster, 4in. diam., 1oz.16dwt.

Charles II circular wine taster, 3¼in. diam., London, 1664, 1oz.18dwt.

Louis XV wine taster with shell thumbpiece, 3¼in. diam., circa 1740, 4oz.4dwt.

Costa Rican volcanic stone metate of concave oval form, 19½in. wide, 1000-1500 A.D.

Khmer sandstone head of Buddha, carved in low relief, circa 12th century, 6¾in. high.

2nd/3rd century A. D. East Roman basalt head of a horse, 14in. long.

Ming dynasty sandstone head, 11in. high.

10th/12th century Central Indian buff sandstone female figure with jeweled girle, 22¼in. high.

11th century Central Indian Matrika group in pink sandstone, 33in. long.

One of a pair of George III ormolu mounted Blue-John solid urns, 10in. high.

One of a pair of early 19th century stone Talbot hounds on sandstone plinths, 50in. wide.

Gray schist stele of Kuan Yin, 26in. high.

Nummulitic limestone head of an Amarna princess, 21cm. high, Egyptian.

14th century Belgian sandstone relief of Two Apostles, one with missing head, 36cm. wide.

10th century black stone stele, 23in. high.

One of a pair of mid 19th century carved stone vases, 24in. diam.

Large sculpture of a pouter pigeon, 1920's, 34.5cm. high, in composition stone.

Central Mexican greenstone mask Teotihuacan III-IV, 18.5cm. high.

Aztec volcanic stone figure, 1300-1500 A.D., 15½in. high.

Arts & Crafts style carpet, designed by C. F. A. Voysey.

Brussels Renaissance tapestry, circa 1540, 11ft.4in. high x 15ft.6in. wide.

17th century Brussels armorial tapestry with arms of the Contreras family, 13ft.3in. x 9ft.

Early 18th century Gobelins tapestry in muted colors. 15ft.2in. x 11ft.3in.

Early 18th century Dutch armorial tapestry cushion cover, 22 x 26in.

19th century Brussels 'Art of War' tapestry by Gaspar van der Borcht, 86 x 94in.

19th century Japanese wall-hanging worked in ivory silk and gray and blue thread, 2.32 x 1.07m.

'Chinoiseries' tapestry by Joshua Morris, circa 1720, 10ft. wide.

19th century wall-hanging in gold and gray thread, 2.20 x 1.52m.

19th century Rescht panel with floral decoration on a madder ground, 9ft.2in. long.

'Chinoiseries' tapestry by Joshua Morris, circa 1720, 13ft. wide.

Early 17th century Florentine red velvet altar hanging embroidered in silks, 75 x 63in.

Large hand-enameled tinplate limousine, probably by Carette, circa 1911, 16½in. long.

French tinplate child's cooking stove complete with utensils, circa 1900, 17½in. wide.

Hubley two-seated brake drawn by a pair of horses, 16½in. long.

French chamois-covered pig automaton, probably by Decamps, circa 1910, 10¼in. long.

Late 19th century American tin kitchen with stove, cupboard and pump, 19in. wide.

Tin wind-up monkey cyclist, circa 1925, 8¾in. high.

Late 19th century American rocking horse with horsehair mane and tail, 47in. long.

American child's pedal car, circa 1925, by Steelcraft, 36in. long.

French 'walking griffon' automaton, circa 1920, 14in. long.

German hand-enameled tinplate duck in original cardboard box, circa 1905, 7in. long.

Bing tinplate tram with clockwork mechanism, circa 1920, 7in. long, slightly rusted.

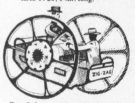

Rare Lehmann 'zig-zag' rocking vehicle with two figures, circa 1910, 5in. wide.

French child's 'galloper' tricycle with applied mane, tail and saddlery, circa 1880, 29in. long.

Bing tinplate monoplane, 1930's.

Cast iron 'Old Dutch' pull toy, America, circa 1925, 9in. long.

Clockwork 'Wheel of Death', Russian, 1896, 9in. high.

English clockwork toy 'Home James', circa 1900.

Wooden fortress, circa 1950, complete with soldiers and animals.

Hand enameled clockwork toy, German, 1900, 6in. high.

Gunthermann clockwork tram, circa 1920, 9½in. long.

Meccano bi-plane construction kit, circa 1933, 1ft.3in. long.

Bing clockwork tinplate two-seater Mercedes, 9½in. long, circa 1912.

Marx tin wind-up 'Tidy Tim', New York, 1933, 9in. long.

Large plush-covered cartoon figure 'Felix the Cat', English, circa 1830, 28½in. high.

Edwardian doll's perambulator with folding hood and boat-shaped body.

German 'Oh-My' tinplate dancer by Lehmann, 10in. high, circa 1925, in original box.

German 'Man on a Pig' toy.

Mickey Mouse organ grinder, about 1930, possibly by Distler, 6in. long.

Two Fun-e-Flex painted wooden toys, Mickey & Minnie Mouse, circa 1931, American, 6¾in. high.

Cast iron model cooking range, American circa 1920 1ft. 1in. wide.

French 'Jeu de Course' game, circa 1900, 10½ x 10½in.

Schoenhuts cracker-jack clown with original box and chair.

Marx clockwork walking Popeye, 8in. high.

Unusual painted lead and papier-mache tea-drinking toy, probably French, circa 1880, 12in. high.

Hess friction drive limousine, 8¼in. long, circa 1920-25.

Mid 19th century Bavarian Noah's Ark, 19in. long, complete with animals.

Gun mounted on a tank chassis by Britain.

Stuffed toy 'Minnie Mouse' by Dean's Rag Book Ltd., circa 1930, 7in. high.

Marx lithographed tin wind-up 'Donald Duck Duet', New York, 1946, in good condition, 9in. high.

Early 20th century German clockwork clown toy, 9in. high.

Early German hand-enameled tinplate carousel, 15¼in. high, circa 1895.

Clockwork 'Boy on a Swing', English, 1937, 3½in. wide.

American set of 'Snow White' picture bricks, circa 1946.

Fine G.G. Kellerman clockwork tinplate frog, German, circa 1930 4¾in. high.

German Arnold tinplate motorcycle, 8in. long, circa 1950.

French Cinematograph-Toy viewer with eight paper bands, circa 1900.

1930's wind-up ice cream tricycle.

German Lehmann 'anxious bride' clockwork toy, circa 1914, 8½in. long.

German acrobatic clown toy.

Distler clockwork organ grinder, circa 1923, German, 7in. high.

Clockwork Steakhouse Joe, made in Japan.

Tinplate clockwork horse and cart, by G. and K. Greppert & Keich, Brandenburg, 17cm. long.

German tinplate clockwork 'Jolly Sambo', 6¾in. high, circa 1920.

Lead set of Snow White and Seven Dwarfs by Britain, 1938.

Stevens & Brown tin mechanical Champion velocipede, patented 1870, 9¼in. high.

Marx lithographed tin wind-up 'Popeye Express', New York, 1935, in original box, 9in. diam.

Printed tinplate dancing couple with clockwork motor, probably French, circa 1905, 8in. high.

A tinplate clockwork landaulette by Georges Carette, about 1910.

Early 20th century pull along barking dog, English, 1ft. 2in. high.

German Phillip Vielmetter painted tin drawing clown, circa 1900, 5½in. high.

Child's pull-along horse covered with pony skin, circa 1850, 11½in. high.

Governess cart by Wade
of Norwich, circa 1900,
10ft. long overall.

Early 19th century velocipede.

Rudge Whitworth tricycle with 5ft.
5in. black frame, circa 1899.

Wooden Victorian
dogcart.

Beautifully restored Romany
Vardo.

A Victorian uphol-
stered bathchair.

Mid Victorian velocipede with
cast iron frame and iron rimmed
wooden wheels.

Reindeer or horse drawn
sleigh, circa 1860, pro-
bably Eastern European.

19th century hand milk
float of iron and wood,
61in. high.

French pastry cook's
van, circa 1900.

Late 18th century hard-topped
surrey with iron rimmed
wheels.

International Baby
Carriage Store child's
pushchair, circa 1900,
48in. long.

English ordinary bicycle,
circa 1880, 4ft.8in.
high.

Early 20th century Ameri-
can wicker baby carriage
with parasol, 56½in. high.

Late 19th century Russian
painted wooden sledge.

19th century four wheel
carriage.

George III mahogany tray inlaid with a conch shell.

Chinese lacquer tray, 2ft.10in. wide, circa 1820, on four bamboo legs.

Rare George I small walnut tray, 1ft.4¾in. wide.

Unusual Galle carved and inlaid fruitwood tray, circa 1900.

Late Victorian mahogany butler's tray with stand.

17th century early Lac Burgaute tray, 13in. diam.

Edwardian mahogany tray and stand with painted decoration.

Large Moreau silvered pewter tray, 45cm. wide, circa 1900.

TSUBAS

Iron tsuba of the Hiragiya school.

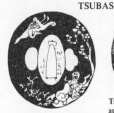

Shakudo Nanako tsuba by Yanagawa Naomasa.

Tsuba of mokko form applied with two spiders, details in silver and gold nunome, 7.9cm. high, signed Chikatoshi.

Higo school tsuba of circular form, 7.3cm. high, unsigned.

Iron tsuba pierced and chiseled with cherry blossoms picked out in gold.

Decorative tsuba of red copper and sentoku plate by Ishiguro Masatsune III.

Rare copper tsuba decorated in katakiri with a pair of Sumo wrestlers.

Well carved iron tsuba, 8.1cm., signed by Kyokusuiken Okabe Tadamasa.

INDEX

INDEX

INDEX

INDEX

INDEX